When Rain Falls

Written by **Melissa Stewart**
Illustrated by **Constance R. Bergum**

PEACHTREE
ATLANTA

For J. L. Bell, who introduced me to the
Society of Children's Book Writers and Illustrators
—M. S.

For my forever friends Kathy and Shelley
—C. B.

Published by
PEACHTREE PUBLISHERS
1700 Chattahoochee Avenue
Atlanta, Georgia 30318-2112
www.peachtree-online.com

Art direction by Loraine M. Joyner
Composition by Melanie McMahon Ives

Illustrations created in watercolor on 100% rag watercolor paper. Title typeset in ITC
Britannic Bold; text typeset in Baskerville Infant.

Printed in Singapore
10 9 8 7 6 5 4 3 2 1
First Edition

Library of Congress Cataloging-in-Publication Data

Stewart, Melissa.
 When rain falls / written by Melissa Stewart ; illustrated by Constance Bergum.-- 1st ed.
  p. cm.
 ISBN-13: 978-1-56145-438-9 / ISBN 10: 1-56145-438-9
 1. Rain and rainfall--Juvenile literature. 2. Animal behavior--Juvenile literature. I.
Bergum, Constance Rummel. II. Title.
 QC924.7S745 2008
 591.72'2--dc22
                          2007031395

Inside clouds, water droplets budge and bump, crash and clump. The drops grow larger and larger, heavier and heavier until they fall to the earth.

When rain falls in your neighborhood,

you run inside and wait for the storm to end.

When rain falls in a forest...

...scurrying squirrels suddenly stop. They pull their long, bushy tails over their heads like umbrellas.

A hawk puffs out its feathers to keep water out and warmth in.

Chickadees stay warm and dry inside their tree hole homes.

A doe and fawn take cover
under a leafy tree canopy.

A red fox family nestles
in a warm, cozy den.

When rain falls on a field...

...plump little caterpillars crawl under leaves and cling to stems. Adult butterflies dangle from brightly colored flower heads.

A raindrop knocks a ladybug off a slippery stem. The insect bounces into the air and then tumbles to the ground.

A spider watches and waits as the rain beats down on its carefully built web.

A mouse crouches under
a fallen leaf.

Bees hide in hives, and
ants stay safe in their
underground nests.

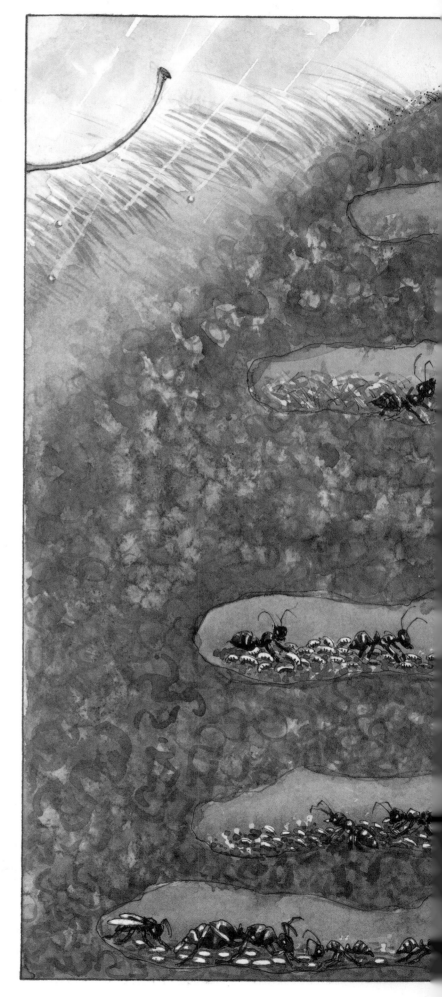

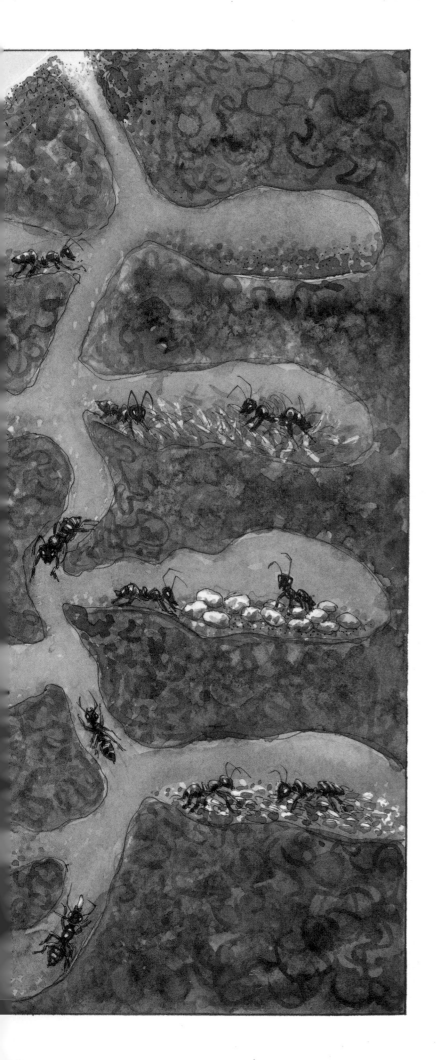

*When rain falls in
a wetland…*

A dragonfly swoops down to perch
below a fluffy cattail seedhead.

Whirligig beetles swim in circles
and struggle to stay afloat.

Sparrows huddle deep inside
a dense cluster of leafy bushes.
But ducks continue to cruise
through the water. Raindrops
slide right off
their oily feathers.

*When rain falls
in a desert…*

...a rattlesnake squeezes into a rocky crevice. It curls up tight and falls asleep.

A tarantula scuttles into
an underground tunnel.

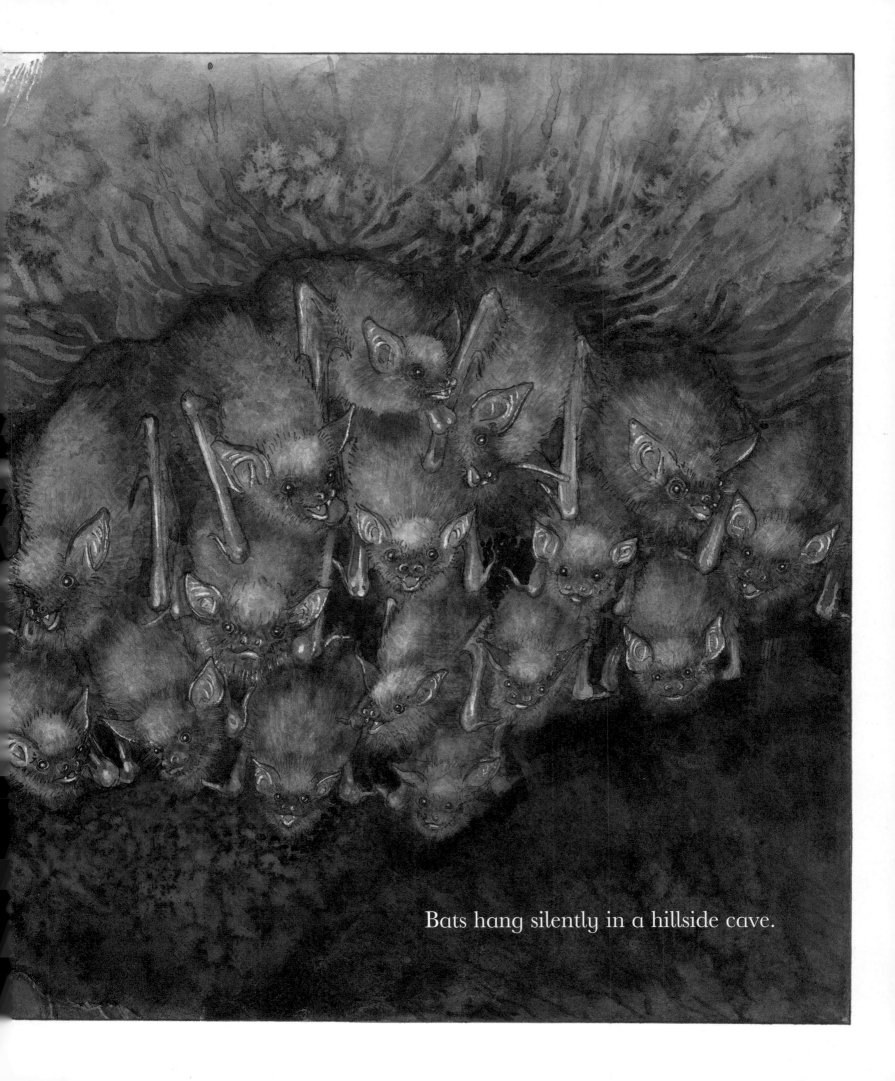

Bats hang silently in a hillside cave.

An elf owl
takes cover
in a cactus
nest.

Spadefoot toads dig to the surface. They mate, lay eggs, and then burrow back into the sand.

When the rain stops…

...animals living in fields and forests, wetlands and deserts return to their daily routines.

And so do you.

The Indian Wars

The
MILITARY HISTORY
of the
UNITED STATES

Christopher Chant

The Indian Wars

MARSHALL CAVENDISH
NEW YORK · LONDON · TORONTO · SYDNEY

Library Edition Published 1992

© Marshall Cavendish Limited 1992

Published by
Marshall Cavendish Corporation
2415 Jerusalem Avenue
PO Box 587
North Bellmore
New York 11710

Series created by Graham Beehag Book Design

Series Editor	Maggi McCormick
Consultant Editors	James R. Arnold
	Roberta Wiener
Sub Editor	Julie Cairns
Designer	Graham Beehag
Illustrators	John Batchelor
	Steve Lucas
	Terry Forest
	Colette Brownrigg
Indexer	Mark Dartford

Library of Congress Cataloging-in-Publication Data

Chant, Christopher.
  The Military History of the United States / Christopher Chant –
Library ed.
     p. cm.
  Includes bibliographical references and index.
  Summary: Surveys the wars that have directly influenced the
United States., from the Revolutionary War through the Cold War.
  ISBN 1-85435-355-1 ISBN 1-85435-361-9 (set)
  1. United States - History, Military - Juvenile literature.
 [1. United States - History, Military.] I. Title.
 t181.C52 1991
 973 - dc20   90 - 19547
                                                  CIP
                                                  AC

Printed in Singapore by Times Offset PTE Ltd
Bund in the United States

The publishers wish to thank the following organizations
who have supplied photographs:

  The National Archives, Washington. United States
  Navy, United States Marines, United States Army,
  States Air Force, Department of Defense, Library of
  Congress, The Smithsonian Institution.

The publishers gratefully thank the U.S. Army Military
History Institute, Carlisle Barracks, PA. for the use of
archive material for the following witness account:

  Page 72-73
  Memoirs of Service, by Charles Varnum.

Contents

When the Civil War ended in 1865, it became clear that the Federal government's decision, made at the beginning of the war, to create an army in which the comparatively few regular units were joined by a much larger number of volunteer units was wise. The units of the regular army were largely unaffected by the end of the war, except that some returned to the frontier region; those of the volunteer army were gradually demobilized, and the volunteer soldiers returned to their homes. The demobilization process was difficult because of the large numbers of men involved. There were enormous logistical problems in mustering them out of the service, and the difficulty of providing storage accommodation for weapons and other equipment.

The regular army faced a series of problems great and small, some new and some old. They included occupation duty in the defeated southern states, the threat of the French in Mexico, a number of upheavals in the North, trouble with various Indian tribes, and, within the regular army itself, a renewal of the old antagonism between field units and staff departments.

Military Isolation

In the period between the end of the Civil War in 1865 and the beginning of the

Major General ''Phil'' Sheridan emerged from the Civil War with a very high military reputation. He continued to build on it in the difficult period after 1865, when he commanded the Department of the West.

The Grand Parade of the Army of the Potomac moves through Washington, D.C., on May 23, 1865. Already the demobilization of the huge Federal army was under way, and the resurgence of limited war on the Indian frontier would have to be met with wholly inadequate forces.

Spanish-American war in 1898, the army and navy were comparatively isolated from the mainstream of American civilian life. However, the army made considerable strides in its development as a professional fighting force. It evaluated many types of new equipment and adopted those that it considered both suitable and affordable. To a lesser extent, it experimented with up-to-date weapons, made feasible by an accelerating pace of technical sophistication. Despite the army's view of itself as an organization at an arm's length from the rest of the United States, it also made valuable contributions to the overall advancement of the United States.

On May 23 and 24, 1865, some 150,000 men of Major General George Gordon Meade's Army of the Potomac and Major General William Tecumseh Sherman's Army of the Tennessee and Georgia paraded through Washington. This Grand Review before President Andrew Johnson and the army's own commanding generals on a review stand on Pennsylvania Avenue marked the end of the army that had won the Civil War. Demobilization of the volunteer units started immediately afterward. Yet the Grand Review served purposes other than honoring the victorious soldiers and their formations. It was a graphic demonstration of the military muscle of the United States, and by implication a confirmation of the industrial and social strengths

behind it. It was meant to impress the leaders of the European powers and the defeated Confederacy alike that the United States was now a major power with a strong central government.

The French Threat in Mexico

Even as the units involved in the Grand Parade were preparing for their triumph, the War Department was responding to the possibility of an external threat. Major General Philip Henry Sheridan, one of the younger generals who had emerged as a highly effective commander in the later stages of the Civil War, was now sent to command American forces west of the Mississippi River and south of the Arkansas River. Sheridan had about 80,000 men under his command. He concentrated 52,000 of them in Texas as military backup for the political pressure that the U.S. government was exerting against French troops in Mexico.

The presence of the French resulted from the Mexican civil war, which began in 1857. After the Battle of Calpulalpam in December, 1860, full control of the country was assumed by a liberal faction under Benito Juarez, whose government had been recognized by the United States on April 6, 1859. Mexico's finances had been completely destroyed by its civil war, and Juarez was forced to suspend payment of foreign debts. To protect their

Even though there had been great improvements in the design and production of American pistols during the Civil War, there were still officers who preferred imported weapons such as this British-made Webley "Longspur" revolver.

interests and to secure payment of money owed to them, France, Spain, and the United Kingdom despatched a joint expeditionary force. It occupied Veracruz in December, 1861, and then moved inland. Spain and the U.K. withdrew their forces in April, 1862. Emperor Napoleon III of France decided that since the United States was occupied with its own civil war, the time was ripe to establish a French puppet state in Mexico. French reinforcements were sent in, and in June, 1863, the Archduke Maximilian, brother of Emperor Franz Josef of Austria-Hungary, was installed as emperor of Mexico. Meanwhile, the Juarist party attempted to regain control of their country in an increasingly bitter guerrilla war.

The United States refused to recognize Maximilian as ruler of Mexico, and at one time provided refuge for Juarez and his senior military commander, General Mariano Escobedo. With the American Civil War in full swing, the U.S. had not been able to do anything except protest at the French presence in Mexico. by May,

1865, this situation had altered; substancial numbers of battle-hardened troops were deployed into Texas within easy march of the frontier with Mexico along the line of the Rio Grande.

Plans drawn up during the Civil War meant that most of them should be demobilized within three months of the war's end. Because of the threat from the French in Mexico and the need to provide occupation forces in the southern states, it was then decided to phase the demobilization of the volunteer units over a period of 18 months or more. By November 15, 1865, more than 800,00 volunteers had been paid, mustered out, and transported home by the Quartermaster Corps. A year later, there were only 11,043 volunteers left in service, most of them men in the Negro regiments, and even they had been demobilized by October, 1867.

Napolean III understood that American demobilization was underway, but he also knew that the process had been slowed and could be reversed if

necessary. This knowledge was emphasized by the presence in France of Major General John McAllister Schofield, who had been sent specially by President Johnson to confirm the U.S. adherence to the "Monroe Doctrine" of non-interference in affairs in the western hemisphere by non-American countries. By the end of 1866, Napoleon III had decided that his Mexican venture was not worth the risk. The finantial return was likely to be poor too, especially as the Juarists were gaining the upper hand in the armed struggle within the country. In February, 1867, the French started to withdraw, but Maximilian decided to stay and fight for his kingdom. Besieged at Queretaro, he was betrayed by one of his own men, captured, court-martialed, and, on June 19, 1867, executed by a Mexican firing squad.

Volunteer Demobilization

The American posture was threatening to the French position in Mexico. However, the threat appeared more menacing than it really was, for a large part of Sheridan's force was composed of volunteers demanding their demobilization. On May 1, 1865, the U.S. Army included 1,034,064 volunteers. General Ulysses Sinpson Grant, the general-in-chief of the U.S. Army, realized that the authorized strength of the regular army was now inadequate for its tasks. The regular army had been kept small during the Civil War, but Grant now proposed that it be expanded to 80,000 men. The concept was opposed by Secretary of War, Edward McMasters Stanton and by Congress. Some increase was inevitable, and on July 28, 1866,

Congress voted in favor of an establishment strength of 54,302 officers and men. At the end of September, 1867, the strength of the regular army reached 57,000 men, the highest level between the end of the Civil War and the beginning of the Spanish-American War.

Difficulties of Recruitment

Recruitment was still as much a problem as it had been before the Civil War, but Grant's task was not eased by Congress's decision in 1869 to cut the number of infantry regiments to 25 and the establishment strength to 45,000 men. Further reduction followed in 1876, when the organization of the regiments was modified to impose a maximum overall strength of 27,442 men. This basic strength continued until the time of the Spanish-American War.

The 1866 Congressional vote also ordained that the regular army should contain six Negro regiments. There were two cavalry regiments and four infantry regiments; though the infantry units were reduced to two regiments during the cuts of 1869.

While its basic organization was being debated and modified in Washington, the army itself was involved in the reconstruction of the southern states. The Civil War had ended all dispute about slavery and states' rights. There now remained the very real task of rebuilding the South and re-forming the victorious northern and the defeated southern states into a single United States. Everyone concerned realized that failure in this immensely difficult task of "winning the peace" would undo all the sacrifices of the Civil War.

Ulysses Simpson Grant
For further references
see pages
10, 11, 42, 43

The Reconstruction of the South

The army was involved right from the beginning. As the federal armies advanced into the Confederacy, the governments of most southern states disintegrated. Thus, the Federal army's provost marshals soon found that their role was extended from policing their own soldiers to policing and, on an increasing basis, administrating whole civilian areas. Soon the duties of the provost marshals extended from basic matters of public hygiene to investigation of southerners' loyalty.

Toward the end of the Civil War, Congress established the Bureau of Refugees, Freedmen, and Abandoned Lands (generally known as ·the Freedmen's Bureau) and placed it under army control for its main task of protecting and aiding former slaves. Late in 1865, most of the army's administrative functions in the southern states were passed to the bureau, which was headed by Major General Oliver Otis Howard, a career officer with a longstanding opposition to slavery.

After the assassination of President Abraham Lincoln in April, 1865, President Johnson pushed ahead with his own plans for reconstruction in the south. In April, 1866, he declared the Civil War officially over, pardoned most former Confederate leaders on the condition that they took an oath of loyalty, and then permitted the re-establishment of civilian government in the southern states. These measures led the army, headed by Stanton and Grant, to look to Congress rather than the president for help in preventing harassment of the Federal forces in the South. A majority of Congressmen were also decisively opposed to Johnson's policy, and Congress enacted a string of legislation to assert its supremacy over the president, undoing Johnson's work and placing the army back in control of the South.

Dispute for Control of the Army

The core of the legislation passed by Congress in 1867 was made up of the Command of the Army Act (part of the Army Appropriations Act), the Tenure of Office Act, and the First Reconstruction Act. The first acts stipulated that presidential orders to the army should be

This drawing reflects the role of the Freedmen's Bureau, under Major General Oliver O. Howard, in raising the educational standards of black people. The bureau was established in 1865 for one year as part of the War Department, and its tasks were obtaining labor contracts, helping to find homes, settling disputes, and raising educational standards. The bureau spread hundreds of agents through the southern states. During its existence, the bureau spent $17,000,000 in establishing more than 100 hospitals, treating 500,000 patients, distributing 20,000,000 rations, settling many thousands of freed slaves on abandoned or confiscated lands, and setting up 4,000 schools.

routed through the Washington office of the general-in-chief, who could be removed only with the approval of the Senate. The second similarly ordained that the approval of the Senate was required before the president could remove members of the cabinet. The first act was intended to make Grant, not the president, supreme commander of the army, while that of the second was to keep Stanton at the head of the War Department. In fact it provided the legal framework for the impeachment of Johnson the following year after he suspended Stanton from office without senatorial approval.

The First Reconstruction Act divided the southern states into five military districts, each headed by a major general who reported directly to Washington. This was an interesting departure from the normal administrative structure of the U.S. Army, which divided the country into geographical regions that were each subdivided into subordinate departments. However, in March 1867 there were only two divisions, those of the Missouri and of the Pacific. The rest of the country was divided into the five southern districts and a number of departments that also reported directly to Washington. As the years passed, the army created more geographical divisions, and in 1870, the Division of the South made up of the five reconstruction districts divided into three territorial departments, appeared.

Though there was considerable debate about whether the First Reconstruction Act took control of the reconstruction forces away from President Johnson, Grant was in no doubt. He informed Sheridan, one of the five district commanders, that he did not need to concern

The scene at the opening of impeachment proceedings against President Andrew Johnson on March 13, 1868. This action was undertaken by a Congress infuriated at Johnson's use of the army in the southern states to promote the rights of black ex-slaves. It ultimately failed by a single vote.

The seven representatives who led the impeachment proceedings included Ben Butler, Thaddeus Stevens and George Boutwell.

White resentment about the situation in the southern states after the Civil War resulted in the establishment of the Ku Klux Klan as an organization dedicated to the ideals that had prevailed in the south before 1865.

himself with the opinion of civil officials. This view was reinforced in the Third Reconstruction Act of July, 1867, which laid down that: "no district commander...shall be bound in his action by any opinion of any civil officer of the United States." The First and Third Reconstruction Acts therefore gave effective control of reconstruction forces to the army under direct Congressional control and left the president in control only of the forces in the territorial divisions and departments.

A Wide Diversity of Army Tasks

The district commanders and their subor-

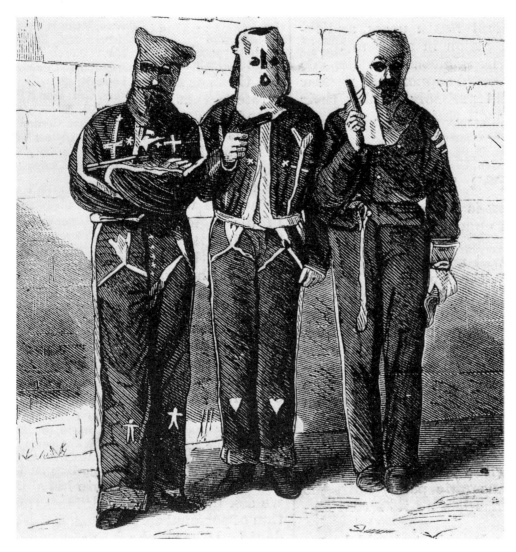

Klansmen captured by Federal authorities in 1870. The organization was rapidly seen as racist and banned.

dinate officers in the southern states controlled matters as diverse as punishment of horse stealing and moonshining, via civil and commercial law, to education and the approval of new state constitutions by voters whose registration they had to administer. The U.S. army achieved its task both successfully and swiftly; by 1870, the process of restoring civil authority to the southern states had been virtually completed. As the states reassumed responsibility for their own affairs, the number of troops needed for occupation duties declined rapidly. The tasks imposed on existing occupation forces were to support civil authority by protecting former slaves and their white supporters, policing elections, maintaining law and order, and keeping the peace between state officials often in conflict with each other.

The single factor that concerned the army and Congress most by 1871 was the rapid growth in the size and impact of the Ku Klux Klan. This white terrorist organization threatened the existing control of the south by a Negro-Radical Republican coalition. The army therefore collaborated with federal marshals in large-scale efforts which helped to check the effect of the Klan, but not to eradicate it. The task should actually have fallen to the restored militia forces in southern states, but as they were made up predominantly of ex-slaves, they were not particularly effective against the Klan, which concentrated a large part of its efforts against these black militiamen. White antipathy to the presence of uniformed black soldiers created so many problems that black militia units were disbanded.

The Army Ends its Task in the South in March, 1877

Rutherford B. Hayes became president after one of the more fraudulent elections in American history. One of the conditions on which the Democrats finally agreed to Hayes's presidency was that occupation forces would be removed from the southern states. In April, the last occupation forces were withdrawn and sent to other areas, and the U.S. Army's part in the reconstruction was over.

Except for the continuing Indian wars and Sheridan's show of strength against the French in Mexico, the U.S. Army was involved in no conventional military operations between the end of the Civil War and the beginning of the Spanish-American War. It was involved, however, in a number of civil disturbances in the southern states and elsewhere. In 1878, Congress banned the use of the army without the authorization of "the Constitution or...Congress" because the army had been employed on hundreds of occasions at the instigation of federal marshals for strike-breaking, local law enforcement, arrest of offenders, and tax collection.

The most celebrated of these occasions was the first major national labor dispute. In the summer of 1877, railroad strikes spread to more than a dozen states. There were many requests for federal aid, and the administration of President Hayes launched a policy of rapid response to protect federal property, when requested by a federal judge or state governor. Almost every post in Major General Winfield Scott Hancock's Division of the Atlantic was stripped of men to create a force bolstered by detachments for other areas, which was further strengthened by elements of the Marine Corps.

Hayes gathered information from a number of sources. One that was particularly valuable was the countrywide network of observer-sergeants at weather stations manned by the U.S. Signals Corps. These men already sent a steady and regular stream of weather reports to Washington; it was a simple matter for them to add information about conditions of local labor relations.

Support for the Civilian Authorities

The federal forces seldom came into contact with mobs during the 1877 strike.

However, "by their presence alone," these small but disciplined bodies of troops played a major part in damping down the ardor of the mobs. The army of the period mustered only 24,000 men, and other commitments meant that only a small part of the complete strength could be used to support the civilian authorities. Even so, the army's part was decisive and resulted in no deaths, civilian or military.

The most controversial use of troops in a labor-relations role also established legal precedents with far-reaching implications. The occasion was the so-called Pullman strike of 1894, a railroad dispute that centered on Chicago, but caused outbreaks in several other parts of the country.

Against the wishes of Governor John Peter Altgeld of Illinois, President Grover Cleveland sent troops to carry out the orders of the federal courts, granted that the mail was not interrupted, and maintain the rule of federal law. This move was opposed by other governors, as well as by Major General Nelson Appleton Miles, commanding the 2,000 soldiers in Chicago. At first, it appeared to be achieving little. The authorities soon realized that the soldiers were being wasted as piecemeal reinforcements for federal marshals and policemen faced with local problems. The units were concentrated under a single command and authorized to fire on any mob, once due warning had been given. On at least one occasion, at Hammond, Indiana, on July 7, 1894, a detachment of troops did fire on a mob that was about to fall on them in overwhelming numbers, killing one rioter and

wounding many others.

Violence in the 1894 strike was far less than that connected with the 1877 dispute, but Major General John Schofield reported that their use as strike-breakers had brought the 28,000-strong army "nearly to the limit" even though they had fulfilled their duties "promptly and effectively." In California, naval and marine troops were also used. The president's decision to send in troops without prior consent from the state was later disputed in law, but the Supreme Court unanimously sustained Cleveland's decision.

Reorganization of the Militia

While the men of the regular army were used on occasion in strikes, this task was more frequently assigned to the state militias, which had existed since the Revolutionary War as the country's only effective militia units. The events of the 1870s made many responsible people consider the possibility of another uprising against federal power, and moves were made to improve militia units with better organization and modern weapons. In 1879, the National Guard Association was founded in St. Louis, Missouri, to support improvement efforts, and between 1881 and 1892, all the states followed the lead of New York in recasting their militia units along National Guard lines.

A part-time military life appealed to many men in the 1870s and 1880s, especially as militia and National Guard units had an element of the fraternity

The Savage Navy percussion-cap revolver was used in the Civil War, and in limited numbers in the West, during the period of the Indian wars. The lower "trigger" was used to cock the hammer, and the upper one to release it. This 0·36-inch caliber weapon was obsolete by the mid-1870s, but was still used by many Indians well into the 1890s.

Chief, Oglala Sioux, 1876.

Seen on an Appaloosa horse, this chief carries a feathered lance and shield, and his clothing and other kit include beaded shirt and leggings, moccasins, a "hair pipe" breastplate, and an eagle-feather bonnet with trailers.

and social club about them. National Guard units enjoyed local prestige in most places, but overall disapproval of the military meant that Congress refused to enact a new militia act. However, pressure from the National Guard Association resulted in 1887 legislation that doubled the federal firearms grant, which had stood at $200,000 a year since 1808.

The industrial development and overall mood of anti-militarism of the last quarter of the 19th century in the United States were major factors in an era that witnessed swift and enormous change. The rapid industrialization of the period sparked the labor movement as industrial workers began to feel their economic and social strength, but this element became prominent only after the turn of the century. Anti-militarism was a far more complex matter. Perhaps it had its origins in the terrible casualties and social upheavals of the Civil War, but it was also connected with the emergence of the United States as a major economic power. Aptly described as "business pacifism," the movement gathered considerable if undefined strength; the military was rejected as outmoded in a world centered on making and selling goods. This whole philosophy took its most virulent forms in an overt hostility to the army and outright opposition to military appropriations. The process increased the already wide gulf between civilians and the military, including the navy as well as the army.

A Gulf between the Military and the Civilian

The divide between the armed forces and the civilian population was physical as well as psychological, since the bulk of the army was on the western frontier fighting Indians. Yet, at its heart, the gulf was emotional and intellectual. The armed forces turned inward and developed a specific military outlook that differed

The location of the main campaigns of the Indian wars after 1865.

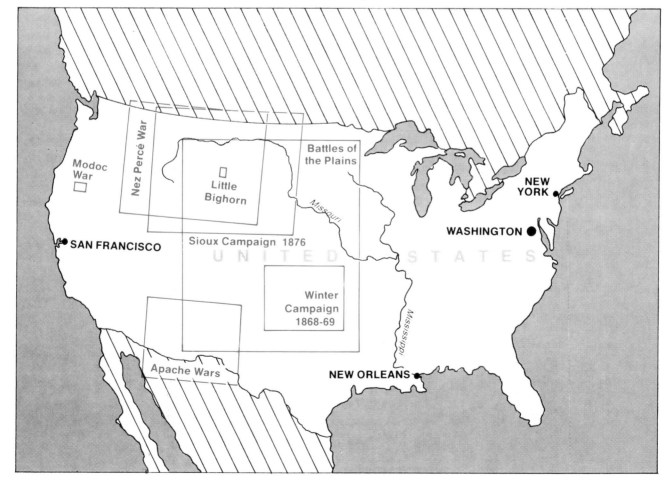

radically from the business pacifism and political liberalism that were the hallmarks of civilian life.

The result was a flowering of true professionalism in the U.S. services. The period after the Civil War has been described as the "most fertile, creative, and formative in the history of the American armed forces." This professionalism was due largely to Rear Admiral Stephen B. Luce in the navy, and of General Sherman and Colonel Emory Upton in the army. Sherman, best remembered as a major figure in the Union's victory in the Civil War, was promoted to full general on March 4, 1869. Four days later he succeeded Grant as commanding general of the army, a position he held until November 1, 1883, when he was succeeded by Lieutenant General Philip Sheridan. Sherman's long tenure in this position was second only to that of Major General Winfield Scott, and Sherman presided over the army throughout the period of developing professionalism. Moreover, Sherman did not follow the example of Grant and two of the other five commanding generals before him in political involvement. He thereby established a tradition of army neutrality in political affairs. As commanding general, Sherman was responsible for the creation of a series of postgraduate military schools where officers learned the finer details of their own branch of the service, and then the principles of higher command.

Upton committed suicide at the age of 42 after learning that he had a fatal disease, but he had been instrumental in preparing a new system of infantry tactics. After extended journeys to assess the armies of Europe and Asia, he urged the creation of a new pattern of an expandable regular army that could absorb large numbers of men for wartime use. Upton reasoned that the militia was inherently inferior to the expandable army, in which wartime volunteers would be commanded by regular noncommissioned and commissioned officers.

During the period between the Civil War and the Spanish-American War, there was also continued controversy between the army and its supporting staff departments. This dispute was as old as the army itself; its origins lay in the legally divided responsibility for all the army's support services. The army simply hoped that the seniority of its commanding generals would provide enough influence to overcome the administrative nightmare that bedeviled its life.

The army argued that its primary task was to fight and that all other activities, such as organization, training, and supply, should be subsidiary to combat efficiency. Reduced to basic terms, the army felt that the profession of arms should control the technical branches that existed only to serve it. By extension, this meant that the commanding general should control the staff.

It was an uphill struggle for the army, and as late as 1895, army regulations still stated that while the military establishment in the territorial commands was controlled by the commanding general in matters of military control and discipline, all associated fiscal affairs were controlled by the secretary of war by means of his various staff departments.

Technical Developments

The same period was marked by considerable, if patchy, technical development within the army. The main hindrances to faster and more extensive progress was a shortage of funds, a lack of inventiveness, and technical conservatism. The greatest progress was made in the field of transportation, especially for operations west of the Mississippi River. The growth of the railroad network there after the Civil War allowed complete wagon trains to be moved rapidly. The wagons were loaded onto flatcars and their mules put into closed cars.

During the Civil War, Henry and Spencer repeating rifles using breech-loaded rimfire cartridges had made considerable contributions, but the main weapon on both sides continued to be the muzzle-loading rifled musket. The advantages of breech-loading weapons were clear, but an overall shortage of funds meant that the Ordnance Department could not even consider the production of such weapons. Instead, it converted large numbers of muzzleloaders for breach loading. This was a poor solution, and in 1872, the

Mississippi River
For further references
see pages
25, 26, 42, 75, 85

army established a board to examine and test existing breech-loading weapons. Over 100 types were evaluated before the army chose the Model 1873 Springfield breech-loading rifle. It used a centerfire cartridge of 0·45-inch caliber, which the Ordnance Department had decided was best suited as the standard type for infantry rifles, cavalry carbines, and pistols. Further improvement of the Model 1873 produced the Model 1889, which was the army's last single-shot rifle firing a large-caliber round with black powder propellant. This weapon was in service with National Guard units as late as 1898.

The Springfield rifle remained in large-scale service even after the adoption of later weapons, despite the fact that a number of overseas armies had opted for repeating rifles using cartridges based on smokeless propellant. American manufacturers were slow to adopt the new propellant despite its advantages of smokeless and progressive burning. Smokeless burning was particularly important, for it prevented the battlefield from being clouded in a pall of smoke during extended battles. Progressive burning was even more important, for it allowed the steady acceleration of the bullet as it passed up the barrel.

After smokeless propellant became generally available in the United States, an 1890 board recommended the adoption of a Danish weapon, the 0·3-inch Krag-Jorgensen with a bolt action and five-round magazine for smokeless rounds. It was adopted by the army in 1892 as the Krag, but production at the Springfield Armory did not start until two years later. Congress first demanded the

This illustration shows American soldiers in the type of khaki uniform worn between 1898 and 1900 and carrying the Krag-Jorgensen bolt-action rifle.

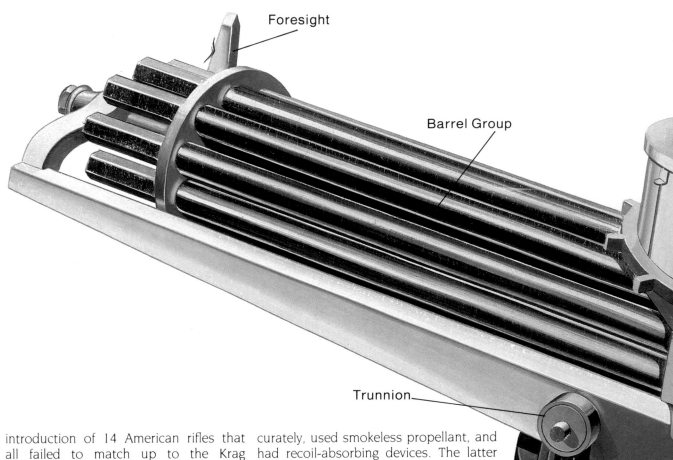

Foresight

Barrel Group

Trunnion

Chambers

introduction of 14 American rifles that all failed to match up to the Krag had been issued throughout the army and by the time production was completed in 1904, the original Model 1892 had spawned two derivatives, the Models 1896 and 1898.

There had been several types of primitive machinegun in the Civil War, but the best was not officially adopted by the army until 1866. It was the Gatling gun, a large weapon that was externally operated by turning a crank. Perhaps because of its size and weight, the army did not consider the Gatling gun a suitable weapon for infantry use. Instead, it was treated as an adjunct of the artillery for tasks such as the defense of bridges and other fixed installations.

Just as it had lagged behind contemporary European armies in adopting repeating rifles firing smokeless cartridges, the U.S. Army also moved more slowly toward the adoption of advanced artillery. By the end of the 19th century, all competent European armies had adopted breech-loading artillery that was capable of firing explosive shells ac-

curately, used smokeless propellant, and had recoil-absorbing devices. The latter prevented the whole weapon from moving with the recoil of the barrel and therefore removed the need for the gun to be relaid between each shot. This opened the way to much higher rates of fire and for indirect fire over longer ranges.

Even so, the army did make progress in the technical sophistication of its artillery. The standard light field piece of the day was the 3·2-inch rifled breech-loading gun. Although they still used black powder propellant, the new guns had rifled steel barrels instead of the smooth-bore iron barrels of earlier weapons. The army also experimented with features such as steel carriages, pneumatic and hydraulic brakes, and a number of mechanical devices for sighting, elevating, and traversing.

Improved Communications

Another field where significant progress was made was in communications. In 1867, responsibility for electric field tele-

Designed by Dr. Richard J. Gatling, who was born in Hertford County, North Carolina, during September 1818, the Gatling gun was a capable though heavy weapon built in several calibers. It was treated as a piece of light artillery as it had to be moved and fired from a two-wheeled carriage. Fed from an overhead hopper or drum, it was operated by an external hand crank, which was later replaced by an electric motor in some models. Operation of the crank rotated the whole assembly of multiple barrels complete with their breeches, whose bolts were each fitted with a cam that fitted into a groove in the stationary breech. As the breech assembly turned, the cams were successively pulled back and allowed to spring forward to complete the cycle of extracting and ejecting the spent case, loading the fresh round, and finally firing the fresh round before returning to the extraction position.

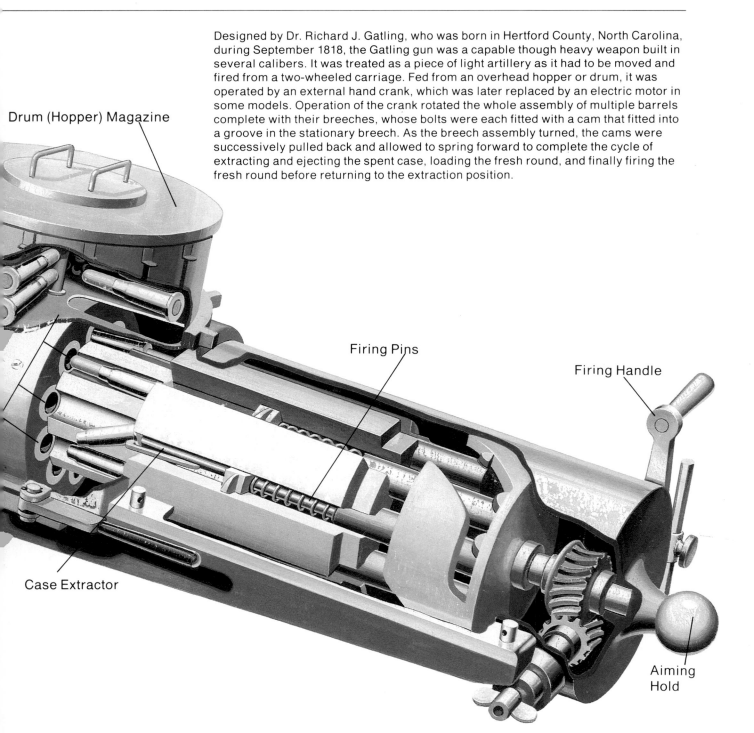

Drum (Hopper) Magazine

Firing Pins

Firing Handle

Case Extractor

Aiming Hold

graphy was restored to the Signal Corps (also known as the Signal Service for many years), from which it had been removed three years earlier. The corps rapidly developed a "flying" field telegraph train using insulated wires, batteries, and sounders. In 1873, the corps acquired much valuable experience in constructing a telegraph line along the east coast for the Life-Saving Service. It then built long telegraph lines in the southwest and northwest to provide communication with otherwise isolated military posts. By 1881, these lines extended a total length of slightly more than 5,000 miles. In the late 1870s, within a couple of years of Alexander Graham Bell's patent for the telephone, the corps was using the device experimentally at its headquarters at Fort Whipple (later Fort Myer) and between this base and Washington. By 1889, a field telephone kit (Bell telephone, Morse key, and battery) had been developed by the corps, but production was slow to start because it was considered too expensive. Even so, by 1892, 59 out of 99 garrisoned posts had telephone equipment either from the Signal Corps or rented from Bell Telephone Company. In the same period, the corps adopted the heliograph, which was very useful in the southwest where sunshine was fairly constant. Experiments were also made with homing pigeons from 1878.

During this period, the army also made an invaluable contribution in a number of civilian fields. When President Johnson's administration bought Alaska from Russia for $7.2 million in 1867, for example, the army occupied the new territory and, through the Department of Alaska, ran the territory until Congress provided the framework for a proper

The United States in the period between 1865 and 1869, when the population grew from 35,700,678 to 39,050,729.

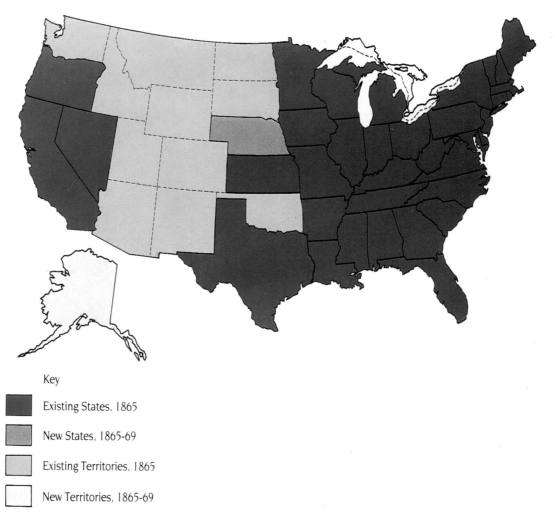

Key

■ Existing States, 1865

■ New States, 1865-69

□ Existing Territories, 1865

□ New Territories, 1865-69

The Corps of Engineers was actively involved in many civil engineering projects throughout this period, including the construction of the Department of the Treasury in Washington, D.C., seen in this Lewis Emory Walker photograph of June 7, 1862.

civilian administration. Over a period of ten years, therefore, the army set up a postal service, maintained law and order, and otherwise administered the territory until its withdrawal from civilian obligations in 1877. After that, the army in Alaska concentrated on exploration. Such expeditions had been started as early as 1869, and later expeditions were as concerned with weather reconnaissance as with actual physical exploration.

Public Works

The army was also actively involved in public works within the United States. The Corps of Engineers played the major role in the development of water resources. Military engineers were responsible for a large number of river and harbor improvements. The navy had primary respon-

sibility for interocean canal surveys, but the United States Isthmian Canal Commission appointed by President Grant in 1872 included Brigadier General Andrew Atkinson Humphreys, the Chief of Engineers, as one of its three members. An engineer officer was also included in the expeditions sent out to survey the Nicaragua and Atrato-Napipi routes in 1874, and in 1897. Colonel Peter C. Hains was one of the members of the Nicaragua Canal Commission appointed by President William McKinley.

The Corps of Engineers was also involved in the design and construction of many public buildings, including the Washington Monument, the State, War, and Navy Building, and what is now the main building of the Library of Congress. The importance of the Corps of Engineers in the development of Washington was reflected in the presidential appointment

June 7th 1862.

of an engineer officer as one of the three governing commissioners of the District of Columbia. Before the establishment of the Interior Department's Geological Survey in 1879, the Corps of Engineers had been responsible for two of the four large-scale surveys of the United States. These were the King Survey of 1867-72, a geological assessment of the 40th parallel, and the Wheeler Survey of 1871- 79, a geological assessment of the region west of the 100th meridian. Both surveys were important to several scientific areas, but while the former was designed to suit civilian rather than military purposes, the latter was really a military survey of the type that had earlier been undertaken by the Corps of Topographical Engineers.

Of all the army's contributions to the overall civil welfare of the United States, the greatest was made by the Medical Department. The role of the army in scientific matters declined in overall terms during the last quarter of the 19th cen-

tury, but this was not true of the Medical Department, whose Army Medical Library (otherwise known as the Surgeon General's Library) and Army Medical Museum were turned by Assistant Surgeon John Shaw Billings into vital sources of basic information and pathology. Another major figure was George Sternberg, who was appointed Surgeon General in 1893 and was a leading light in the science of bacteriology.

The Regular Army Returns to the West

These changes reduced the army from its vast size in the Civil War and then molded its regular peacetime establishment into the pattern it would retain until the end of the 19th century. Meanwhile, the majority of American soldiers were deployed in the west, where they found much fighting. Here, their foes were Indian tribes who

The single greatest spur to westward migration was the discovery of gold in California. This is a typical scene at a prospectors' camp.

had first come into large-scale contact with the whites only 15 years earlier.

Four particular events set the scene for the trouble that was to come. The first was the annexation of Texas in 1845; the second was the treaty with Britain in 1847 that settled the Oregon frontier. The third was the American victory in the Mexican War in 1848, and the fourth the discovery of gold in California during 1849. The first two prompted increasing friction with local tribes, but the third and fourth events were more important. Victory over Mexico added vast areas to the southwestern and western United States, including large regions that were opened up to settlement by families from the east. The gold rush produced a flood of people (both would-be miners and those wanting to exploit their wealth) to California. Many of those bound for California traveled by ship around Cape Horn, but most went overland through the areas ceded by Mexico. A large number of the overland travelers did not reach California, but chose instead to settle at points along the way.

In general, therefore, the nature of the Indian wars was established by the pattern of settler intrusion, Indian reaction, and counter-reaction with considerably greater strength by the settlers. Up to this time, the scope of the Indian wars had been limited by the willingness of the Plains Indians, under pressure from settlements or facing military defeat, to pull back into the open western regions to their rear. By the 1850s, this escape valve was becoming unavailable. The Plains Indians (and increasingly the Indians of the Northwest) were now sandwiched between non-Indian settlement in California and Oregon, which was spreading to the east, and European settlement moving westward from the Mississippi River. The Indian tribes could no longer fall back into relatively empty lands, and the herds of buffalo, on which many of the tribes of Plains Indians relied for their very lives, were being sharply reduced.

In the circumstances, the option facing the tribes was surrender or fight. Many chose to fight. For a period of about 25 years, the tribes resisted in the plains, mountains, and deserts of the west in a series of guerrilla wars. Skirmishes led to pursuits, pursuits led to massacres, massacres led to raids, raids led to expeditions, expeditions led to campaigns, and campaigns led to battles, all in a bewildering assortment of sizes and intensities.

The westward migration inevitably brought settlers into contact and friction with the Indians of the Great Plains. This illustration shows Indians in wolf skins hunting their most important prey, the buffalo, which gave them meat, fat, sinew, bone, horn, and fur-covered skin.

A Poverty of Cavalry

Congress, with no clear appreciation of the real nature of either the Indians or the great plains, thought that the existing army, with its preponderance of infantry and artillery was adequate. At the time, there were only three mounted units, the 1st and 2nd Regiments of Dragoons, which had been raised in the 1830s, and the Regiment of Mounted Riflemen, created in 1846 for service in the Mexican War. However, it was abundantly clear to those with experience of the west that a much larger proportion of mounted men would be needed. As Colonel George Archibald McCall, the Inspector General, reported after a tour of army posts in New Mexico: "I am persuaded that the nature of the service to be required of the Army for the next ten years will be such as to require that the cavalry arm shall greatly predominate in its organization."

Cavalry was, of course, considerably more expensive to outfit and run than infantry. Cavalry needed large numbers of horses, and these horses were costly. So was the feed needed by the horses. Indian ponies could make do with the poor grass of the region, but cavalry horses needed grain that first had to be bought in prosperous regions, where the cost was high, and then transported at additional expense to every "front-line" horse unit. Thus cavalry had the twin disadvantages, as far as a cost-conscious Congress was concerned, of high purchase cost followed by high operating cost.

In the short term, therefore, the army had to make do with its three existing horsed regiments. At the beginning of the 1850s, the 1st Dragoons and the Mounted Rifles were despatched to the Pacific coast. The task of policing the plains fell on the 2nd Dragoons.

Campaigns in the 1850s

In the 1850s, the army deployed between 16,000 and 17,000 men to deal with the tribes west of the Mississippi River. During the decade, there were 30 campaigns against these tribes. The army distinguished 22 of them as "wars." On the plains, trouble was comparatively slow to develop, so the army's first major conflict with the Indian tribes west of the Mississippi River occurred in the northwest. Here, between 1851 and 1858, three campaigns were necessary to subdue the Coeur d'Alenes and Yakimas. Yet they were only the openers to a series of campaigns in the Great Plains and the southwest that involved small-scale but bloody fighting against tribes such as the Apache, Arapaho, Cheyenne, Comanche, Kiowa, Mojave, Navajo, and Sioux. In 1857 alone, the army reported 37 campaigns and expeditions involving combat, and a considerably larger number that involved no fighting.

The experience of the 2nd Dragoons on the Great Plains in the 1850s encapsulates the Indian fighting of the period. Authorized on May 23, 1836, as the 2nd Regiment of Dragoons, this unit was

Like the rifle of the same name and period, the Volcanic pistol of 1854 was limited by its cartridge, which consisted of a bullet with a hollow base containing the black powder charge held in place by a cardboard disk that contained the primer. More successful was the tubular magazine located under the barrel, with a spring to push the rounds back toward the platform that lifted the rearmost round up to a point behind the breech ready for chambering and firing. This type of magazine was used with a different and most successful type of round, with a metal cartridge, on the excellent Henry, Spencer, and Winchester rifles.

redesignated the Regiment of Riflemen on March 5, 1843, but reverted to its original name on April 4, 1844. On August 3, 1861, it became the 2nd Cavalry Regiment. The regiment's service in the Indian wars included New Mexico (1852 and 1854), Wyoming (1866-67), Kansas (1869), and Montana (1870, 1872, 1879, and 1880), the campaigns against the Nez Perce, Bannock, Cheyenne, and the 1876 war against the Sioux.

Trouble with the Sioux on the Platte River

In 1855, a party of Sioux robbed a stagecoach and shot the operator of a ferry boat on the Platte River. A small detachment of the 2nd Dragoons, under the command of Brevet 2nd Lieutenant John L. Grattan, was sent to find and arrest those responsible, but was itself caught by the Indians. All the cavalrymen were massacred. A larger part of the regiment was then gathered at Fort Phil Kearny, Nebraska, along with infantry and artillery, under the dragoons' command-

ing officer, Colonel William A. Harney. Led by the dragoons under Lieutenant Colonel Philip St. George Cooke, this more substantial force set out to punish the Sioux raiders. About half of the Sioux surrendered as soon as they realized the size of the force coming after them, but the rest fled.

The troops found the Sioux camp and, after a night march on September 2, surrounded it with the infantry on one side and the dragoons on the other. The Indians spotted the infantry, struck their camp, and prepared to move away from the infantry straight toward the dragoons' ambush position. The infantry opened fire from one side, and the dragoons then charged from the other. The Sioux managed to extricate themselves in part from this trap, but in the fight and the following cavalry pursuit, they lost 85 killed and five wounded. The army lost four killed, seven wounded, and one missing. In the abandoned Sioux camp, the army found papers from the stagecoach, clothing stripped from the corpses of Grattan's men, and the scalps of two white women.

Apprehensions about the Indians were kept at a high level by illustrations such as this, depicting the massacre of the Oatman family by Apaches in 1851.

Harney sent his prisoners back under escort to Fort Phil Kearny and led the rest of his command northeast into the heart of Sioux territory. The march reached Fort Pierre on the Missouri River on October 20. Not one Sioux was seen during the march, but the surviving raiders were so impressed by Harney's strength and persistence that they surrendered at Fort Laramie on October 25. In March, 1856, Harney signed a peace treaty with the Sioux.

The success of the Harney expedition was valuable ammunition for those trying to persuade Congress that, although cavalry was undoubtedly more expensive to outfit and run than infantry, it was nevertheless cost effective in the operations against the tribes. On March 3, 1855, two more cavalry regiments were authorized as the 1st and 2nd Cavalry Regiments. These became the 4th and 5th Cavalry Regiments in 1861 when all mounted regiments were redesignated as cavalry: the 1st Dragoons became the 1st Cavalry, the 2nd Dragoons became the 2nd Cavalry, and the Mounted Rifles became the 3rd Cavalry.

The Cheyennes Take the War Path

Next to be tackled by the cavalry were the Cheyenne, who had already started a small-scale campaign of harassment of settlers. Early in 1856, they stopped the Salt Lake mail coach and wounded the driver, and one and a half companies of the new 1st Cavalry were despatched under Captain George H. Stewart to catch the offenders. ("Companies" did not become "troops" in American cavalry outfits until 1883.) The soldiers found the Cheyenne camp on the Platte River and charged into it, killing 10 Cheyennes and wounding another ten. The rest of the party escaped and regrouped, harassing Stewart's detachment as it returned. The Cheyenne leaders realized, however, that the writing was on the wall and signed a treaty in which they agreed to leave the Platte River area and stop their attacks on settlers.

This did not suit some members of the tribe, however, and during the winter of 1856-57, they planned to resume their raids in the spring. This information reached the 1st Cavalry's commander, Colonel Edwin Vose Sumner, who decided to pre-empt any trouble. Starting late in May, 1857, he took his regiment, reinforced with two companies of the 2nd Dragoons and some infantry, into Cheyenne country. He divided his command between Lieutenant Colonel Joseph Eggleston Johnston (four companies of

Cheyenne Indians
For further references see pages
30, 36, 37, 45, 46, 48, 49, *51, 52,* 54, 55, 56, 57, 58, 59, 60, 62, 65, 87, 88, 90, *108, 109*

Corporal, 2nd Dragoon Regiment, U.S. Army, 1854.

In 1854 the uniform of mounted regiments underwent several modifications. The most obvious, replaced because the use of inferior dyes caused uneven fading, was the wide band on the shako. It was changed to a narrow welt the color of the facing above a dark blue band. The result was a more uniform appearance when the regiment was on parade. Another major change was the reintroduction of the uniform jacket. Brass epaulets, or shoulder scales, were still worn with the jacket, but were often left behind when units moved into the field. Other items of field clothing were civilian chaps or leggings, and civilian knives carried on the sword belt.

Travelers fend off an attack by Comanche Indians by making a circle to form a corral.

the 1st Cavalry and two companies of infantry), Major John Sedgwick (four companies of infantry), and himself (the rest of his regiment and the two dragoon companies).

On June 29, Sumner's detachment encountered a party of 300 mounted Cheyenne warriors near Greeley, Colorado. In one of the few authenticated uses of the tactic, the Cheyenne formed a battle line with their left wing on the bank of the Solomon River and their right wing on the bluffs at the edge of a valley to the north. Sumner formed his own men in line and led them into the attack, first trotting and finally galloping as the charge neared the Cheyenne line. The Cheyenne had expected the cavalry to use carbines and therefore prepared "medicine" against it, but were completely unnerved by the sight of sabers. Hesitating for only a moment, they turned and ran. The cavalry pursued them for nine miles, killing nine Cheyenne, but twenty of their men were impaled by arrows, and Lieutenant J.E.B. Stuart wounded in the chest by a pistol shot. Thoroughly tired by the pursuit, the cavalrymen returned to the site of the "battle" and camped. Two days later, they found and burned an abandoned Cheyenne village, headed for the Arkansas River, and finally reached Bent's Fort. They received orders to end the campaign, and the troops were sent to Utah. Sumner predicted that the Cheyenne would see the company's withdrawal as a lack of determination and caused more trouble during the summer. During the following winter, however, the Cheyenne came to the conclusion that their efforts of the year had been wasted, and for the next six years, the Cheyenne remained at peace.

The Comanche and Kiowa in Texas

These early campaigns on the plains were mirrored in Texas, where the Comanche and Kiowa were terrorizing the southern plains. In December, 1855, Colonel Albert Sidney Johnston's 2nd Cavalry arrived in Fort Belknap to replace the Mounted Rifles, who were moving to New Mexico. The cavalrymen fought with such determination and skill that the problem was brought under control, but not completely eliminated. Over the following four years, the 2nd Cavalry fought no fewer than 40 small actions with the Indians.

Kiowa Indians
For further references see pages
32, 33, 48, 51, 52, 54, 55, 56

Comanche Indians
For further references see pages
32, 33, 48, 56

Sergeant, Infantry, U.S. Army, 1872.

Seen in campaign dress, this noncommissioned officer is wearing the Model 1872 fatigue hat and the Model 1872 fatigue blouse. The hat was fitted with hooks and eyes so that the brim could be held up at front and back to create headgear that resembled the bicorn of 60 years earlier, and the blouse proved so unpopular that it soon passed from service. The weapon is a Model 1868 Springfield, which was normally associated with a cartridge box on the right hip. This NCO also has two stripes on the lower part of his sleeves. The red stripe means he served in the Civil War, and the white stripe marks five years of service.

Despite the relative success of the 2nd Cavalry, it was clear that protecting the Texas frontier was too great a task for a single regiment. In 1858, the state reconstituted the Texas Rangers, first raised in 1836, with the primary task of fighting the Indians. On May 11, 1858, the Texas Rangers surprised a Comanche village on the Canadian River near Antelope Hills and fought a seven-hour battle. The Comanches lost 76 killed and about 300 more were put to flight in the worst defeat they had suffered so far. Yet the Comanches were far from crushed and returned to their raids with redoubled determination.

The 2nd Cavalry had been scheduled to move to Utah, where the "Mormon War" was underway. It was instead ordered to remain in Texas under the command of Colonel David Emanuel Twiggs to deal with the new Comanche raids. Twiggs organized an expedition based on four companies of his cavalry and a detachment of infantry to serve as base guard, and departed from Fort Belknap on September 15, 1858. On October 1, this force found a Comanche village near Rush Spring and charged. The Comanches were taken by surprise, but reacted so swiftly that they were able to hold off the cavalry for 90 minutes as the women and children escaped. Only then did the Comanche warriors break their holding action and fall back. The Comanche losses were 56 warriors and two women killed, as well as 25 warriors mortally wounded. The 2nd Cavalry's detachment captured 300 horses and burned 20 lodges in the village.

The regiment maintained a series of constant patrols during the following winter, but did not fight a single Comanche party. A squadron of the 1st Cavalry was detached to Fort Arbuckle to reinforce the 2nd Cavalry.

The 2nd Cavalry's major campaign of 1859 began on April 30, when six companies set off up the Arkansas River to find and destroy the Comanches. Two weeks later, the cavalry found a Comanche village at Crooked Creek. This time the cavalry's tactical plan was more sound: mounted men were sent into the hills behind the village to cut all lines of escape, and dismounted skirmishers then moved in drenching rain into the village from the front. The Comanches again fought a spirited rearguard action from every piece of cover they could find, but they were completely trapped and no one escaped. They suffered 49 killed and five wounded, and 32 women and five men were captured. Army losses were two cavalrymen and four Indian scouts killed, and 14 cavalrymen wounded.

A major effort against the Comanches was planned for 1860 and, in preparation for this, during September, 1859, the 1st Cavalry built Fort Cobb, at the junction of Pond Creek and the Washita River.

Failure of the 1860 Campaign

This major expedition against the Comanches and Kiowa was based on advances by four separate columns. Under the command of Major Sedgwick were four companies of the 1st Cavalry and two companies of the 2nd Dragoons from Fort Riley, Kansas. This column achieved little during a substantial reconnaissance south of the Arkansas River to Antelope Hills and then west to the foot hills of the Rocky Mountains. Only one clash occurred during the column's movement, resulting in the death of two Kiowas.

Under the command of Captain Samuel Davis Sturgis was a detachment of the 1st Cavalry that headed north from Fort Cobb on June 6. They encountered a large party of Kiowas at Solomon's Fork, Kansas, but most of the warriors escaped after an inconclusive skirmish when the cavalry were prevented from pursuing by a courageous Kiowa rearguard action.

Under the command of Major Charles F. Ruff (soon replaced by Captain Andrew Porter) were six companies of the Mounted Rifles. Departing from Fort Union, New Mexico, this detachment scouted the plains east of the Canadian River. The nearest it came to Indians was an abandoned village. The last column consisted of the 2nd Cavalry. It left Texas toward the headwaters of the Concho and Colorado rivers, where a small fight took place with 11 Comanches, one of whom was killed.

This major effort of 1860 therefore achieved little in the fight against the

Comanches and Kiowas. The defense of the Santa Fe Trail was improved, however, and Fort Rise was constructed at Big Timbers.

When the Civil War broke out in 1861, the nature of operations in the West changed. The 1st Cavalry, for example, only just escaped capture by fleeing to Fort Leavenworth, Kansas, when Texas seceded from the Union on March 4, 1861. Congress understood that a larger regular army would be needed in addition to the mass of volunteer units that finally emerged. On May 3, 1861, it authorized a 3rd Cavalry Regiment, which became the 6th Cavalry when all the mounted regiments were designated cavalry on August 3, 1861. These six regular units were needed for service in the Civil War and pulled out to the east, leaving the plains stripped of cavalry defense.

Yet a breathing space was made for the creation of new regiments. The outbreak of the Civil War caused the removal of the regular regiments, and the westward flood of settlers virtually stopped. Many states raised volunteer regiments for service on the frontier, but the establishment of these new units was not really put in hand until the fall of 1861. None of the new units was ready for service until the following year, and it was mid-1862 before the plains frontier was adequately protected again. By the time the Civil War ended in 1865, there were 20,000 men in volunteer regiments along the frontier.

The Sioux of Minnesota Rise

The first major Indian trouble after the start of the Civil War flared up in August, 1862. A party of Wahpeton Sioux killed five settlers in Minnesota before destroying the Redwood Agency as well as attacking Fort Ridgely and the town of New Ulm. Unable to take the fort and the town, the Indians laid siege to them until they were

The execution of 38 Sioux Indians at Mankato, Minnesota, on December 26, 1862, at the end of the uprising of the "Farmer" Sioux and "Blanket" Sioux. Under the command of Brigadier General H. H. Sibley, a Federal brigade captured more than a thousand of the Sioux, and condemned 303 of them to death. President Abraham Lincoln reviewed the cases and confirmed the sentences of 39, of whom 38 were hanged on this gallows.

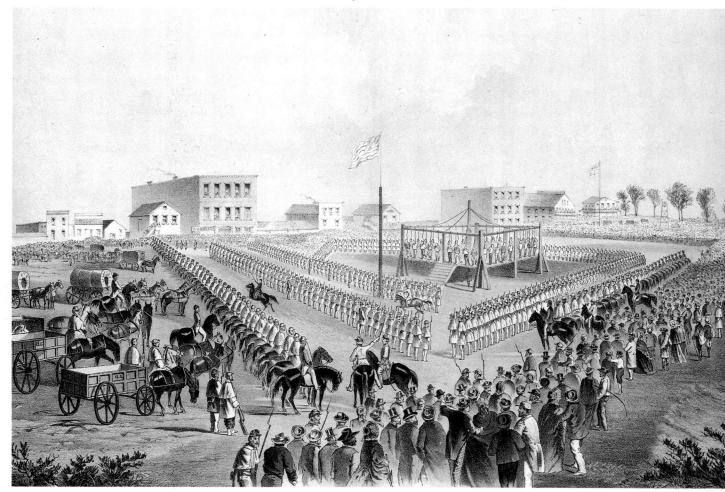

driven off in the Battle of Birch Coulee on September 3, 1862, by newly arrived volunteer infantry with a company of volunteer mounted rangers.

The problem of the Sioux in Minnesota was clearly not over, and additional volunteer infantry was called in. The resulting Battle of Wood Lake was a serious defeat for the Sioux, and the military enthusiasm of the Indians declined rapidly. By October 1862 the Sioux war in Minnesota was over. Yet the settlers destroyed their chance of securing a stable future by hanging 38 of the Indians they had captured. Most of the Sioux leaders had evaded capture, and they moved northwest into the Dakota Territory.

A volunteer brigade was organized to pursue the Sioux who had escaped. Made up of the 1st Minnesota Mounted Rangers, three volunteer infantry regiments, and a battery of volunteer artillery, this force overtook a party of Sioux on July 24, 1863, on the site of what is now Bismarck, North Dakota. The volunteer infantry broke through the lines of Sioux warriors several times, and the Indians then fled, with the volunteer cavalry in pursuit until nightfall. Two days later, the brigade found and burned a Sioux village. The next day, as the brigade was marching toward Stony Lake in pursuit of the Indians, the Sioux main strength fell on the head of the column. The Indians were repulsed with heavy losses and fell back toward Missouri. The brigade reached Stony Lake before turning back to Minnesota.

The Battle of Whitestone Hill

The threat posed by the Sioux was still considerable, and Brigadier Alfred Sully, commanding the Department of Dakota, was given the 6th Iowa and 2nd Nebraska Cavalry to score a decisive victory. On September 3, 1863, four companies of the 6th Iowa encountered about 4,000 Indians camped near the site of present-day Ellendale, North Dakota. The Sioux spotted the advancing horsemen and rapidly surrounded them. One man managed to slip away with a report for Sully, who charged with the rest of the brigade and drove the Sioux into a ravine. The Indians checked the cavalrymen until nightfall, and then slipped away, leaving 3,000 warriors dead, wounded, and captured. The cavalry suffered only 22 killed and 50 wounded, and this Battle of Whitestone Hill was the worst defeat ever suffered by the Sioux at the hands of the cavalry.

Sully knew that the Sioux problem was still far from over, and he launched a major search and destroy operation along

In 1869, the Smith & Wesson 0·44-inch caliber revolver was the first breech-loading revolver adopted by the U.S. Army. This Model 3 weapon was a hinged-frame design that hinged open on a pivot at the lower front edge of the cylinder to provide access to the six chambers as the barrel dropped and the cylinder rose above the single-action hammer mechanism. As seen here, it could be fitted with a shoulder stock to provide greater accuracy over longer ranges.

the Missouri River in July, 1864. By this time, his original two regiments had been reinforced by the 7th Iowa Cavalry, the 2nd Minnesota Cavalry, Brackett's Minnesota Cavalry Battalion, two companies of Dakota cavalry, some infantry, and a small detachment of artillery.

The Sioux, still suffering from their devastating losses at Whitestone Hill in the previous year, appreciated that they could not withstand Sully's reinforced strength. They therefore made for the wild country between the Missouri and Yellowstone rivers in the hope that Sully would be shaken off or deem it too dangerous to follow.

The Battle of Killdeer Mountain

Sully was not deterred, however. On July 28, he found a party of 1,600 Sioux at a village on Killdeer Mountain. The country was too difficult for mounted men, so Sully ordered his cavalry to dismount and form into squares. The Sioux attacked these

squares on the front, flanks, and rear, but the Americans advanced steadily toward the village. The Sioux then formed a skirmish line to buy time for the evacuation of their women and children, but this line was broken by a saber charge launched by Brackett's battalion, which had remained mounted. In the following melee, the Sioux lost 31 killed and the Americans five killed as well as ten wounded. Most of the Sioux escaped, and Sully ordered the destruction of their village on the grounds, as he later wrote, that "I would rather destroy their supplies than kill fifty of their warriors."

Sully's force then pushed farther west into Yellowstone country. It was a difficult time for the American force, which was short of food and found very little water. Sully's detachment reached the Yellowstone River on August 12, and then marched down river to Fort Union, North Dakota, on the Missouri river. The detachment then moved to Fort Berthold and Fort Rice at the end of a campaign that had both badly beaten the Sioux and pushed the frontier farther west.

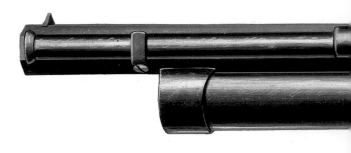

The Le Mat was a nine-shot, double-barrelled percussion-cap pistol developed in New Orleans, but made in Paris, France, by Dr. (or Colonel) J. Alexandre F. Le Mat. The upper barrel fired the eight 0·44-inch rounds carried in the revolving cylinder, and the lower barrel carried a single 0·60-inch charge. The type was much favored in the south during the Civil War, and some weapons survived into the period of the Indian Wars.

The End of "Honorable" Campaigning

Until this time, the campaigns against the Indians had been fought by regular units of the U.S. Army and then by some of the early volunteer units. The discipline of these units meant that the campaigns were generally fought along "honorable" lines, though there were atrocities committed by each side. As regular units were moved east for the Civil War, though, their place was taken by some later volunteer units with much lower standards of discipline. A change occurred in the character of the frontier wars, especially on the Great Plains, and established a pattern of ferocity that was to appear time and again in the following 20 years.

In 1862 and 1863, there was a lull in the fighting in the central area of the Great Plains, where protection for the settlers was provided by volunteer cavalry from California, Kansas, and Ohio. In 1864, tribal unrest once again stirred in a series of small raids in Colorado. Colonel John M. Chivington, commanding the 1st Colorado Cavalry, responded with an appalling plan to "burn villages and kill Cheyennes wherever and whenever found." The American activity that followed not only failed to cure the Cheyenne problem. Worse, it failed to eliminate it and served mainly to inflame the already angry Indians.

Chivington maintained a defensive position with his own regiment, the 11th Ohio Cavalry at Forts Laramie and Halleck, the 7th Iowa Cavalry at Forts Kearny and Cottonwood, and the newly arrived 7th Nebraska Cavalry. For offensive operations, he organized a brigade at Fort Kearny containing the 1st Nebraska, 7th Iowa, and 16th Kansas Cavalry and sent them off on a search-and-destroy operation against the Cheyenne. The search failed to find any opposition, but the Cheyenne had decided that further fighting was pointless. They sent a party to negotiate peace terms; Chivington and the administration of Colorado were not interested.

Chivington's Sand Creek Massacre

Chivington also had at his disposal the 3rd Colorado Cavalry, a volunteer unit raised mainly from the roughest of the frontier bars in Denver, Colorado. The 100-day enlistment of this unit was almost up, and Chivington decided to use the regiment at least once as part of a program dismally summarized in his own words by the sentence "I want no peace till the Indians suffer more." On November 29, 1864, Chivington launched this low-quality unit into a village of Black Kettle's band of Cheyennes on Sand Creek, despite the fact that the village was flying both a white flag and the American flag. The Sand Creek Massacre, as the episode became known, resulted in the deaths of large numbers of Cheyenne (between 70 and 300 were quoted), of whom only 30 were men of

warrior age. The 1st Colorado Cavalry was also present, but refused to take any part in the massacre ordered by Chivington.

This episode was largely responsible for the increasing ferocity with which the Plains tribes fought in the following 20 years. The Joint Committee on the Conduct of the War investigated the massacre and concluded that Chivington "deliberately planned and executed a foul and dastardly massacre which would have disgraced the most savage among those who were the victims of this cruelty."

Renewed war on the plains

The result was inevitable. The Brule Sioux, Northern Arapaho, and Southern Cheyenne immediately took the offensive against all aspects of the white presence in their areas. Every regiment in the region had its hands full as the army tried to stem the tide of Indian anger. On February 6, 1865, about 120 men of the 7th Iowa and 11th Ohio Cavalry were engaged by a very large body of Indians,

but managed to fight their way out of the attack. On February 7, the town of Julesburg, Colorado, was burned down. On February 8, the cavalry again met the war party, this time at Rush Creek, and held its own only by digging in and using the rapid fire possible with its breech-loading Smith and magazine-fed Spencer carbines. Severe weather then put a halt to further military operations in the area.

Farther south, the defense of Texas was left to the Texans; the Confederacy could not spare any of its forces for the task. Texas raised several regiments for frontier defense. Most of them were nominally cavalry regiments, but many in fact served as infantry units. In December, 1864, scouts found evidence that a large force of Indians had entered Texas. A brigade of volunteers and militiamen was alerted to pursue this party, and a 380-man detachment found evidence that a 4,000-man force of Kickapoos was camped in a 100-acre thicket on Dove Creek. The Texans planned to trap the larger Indian force by dividing their own strength: 161 men were to capture the Indian horses and then drive across the

Sioux portraits: On the left is a Chippewa chief in Sioux costume; on the right, a Sioux warrior, Waneta.

creek, while the other 219 were to charge straight into the Kickapoo camp.

The Trap at Dove Creek

Unfortunately for the Texans, it was an elaborate trap. The men who charged into the camp found it deserted. They were surrounded by 500 Indians, who engaged them with British 1853 pattern rifled muskets, while the men entrusted with seizing the Indian horses were driven off by another group of warriors. Both Texan parties tried to flee, but found themselves caught in crossfire. By the middle of the afternoon, the position of both groups of Texans was desperate. The two groups managed to link up and, with about 35 wounded men, managed to cross the creek about 30 minutes before nightfall. The Indians charged the Texas rear, and the Texans retired in complete disorder with the war party in hot pursuit. Only the arrival of a violent storm prevented the Indians from scoring an even greater success. The Texans suffered 36 killed and 100 wounded, and the blow to Texan confidence was considerable.

Meanwhile, the Sand Creek Massacre and the Indian violence that followed it were affecting the central region of the Great Plains. It was clear to the army at the beginning of the spring of 1865 that a major effort would be needed to avoid any repetition of earlier mistakes and their repercussions. The overall plan called for the use of several columns for co-ordinated strikes at the Indians.

Under the command of Brigadier General James Hobart Ford, a force of 1,200 cavalrymen would attack the tribes south of the Arkansas River. Under Sully's command, another 1,200 cavalrymen would push across Dakota north of the Black Hills to build a fort on the Powder River. Another 2,000 cavalrymen under Brigadier General Patrick Edward Connor, would strike at the tribal encampments along the Powder River and cooperate with Sully's force.

Before the campaign started, the Civil War ended. Many of the volunteers began calling for their demobilization, but Ford began his part of the operation on April 29 with the 2nd Colorado Cavalry and parts of the 7th Iowa and 11th Kansas Cavalry. The Arkansas River was too deep to be forded when Ford's column reached it, but despite that, and the mustering out of many of his volunteers on October 1, Ford managed to achieve enough success for the southern tribes to sign a peace treaty on October 4. The peace did not suit all the Sioux, however, notably the Yaktonais and Tetons, as well as those raiding around Fort Laramie.

On July 11, 137 men of the 7th Iowa Cavalry ran into a party of 2,000 Sioux and in a short firefight killed between 20 and 30 Sioux for the loss of four of their own men killed and another four wounded. A 234-man detachment of cavalry from the California, Kansas, and Ohio regiments was sent in pursuit, but 103 of them returned within three days because of foundered horses. On June 17, the other 131 were surprised as they were eating breakfast. The Sioux ran off with their horses, and they had to return on foot after burning their saddles.

The Fight for the Platte Bridge Station

Late in July, the Indians launched a major effort against the Platte Bridge Station (now Casper, Wyoming), which was held by a detachment of the 11th Kansas and 11th Ohio Cavalry. They were backed up by the 6th U.S. Volunteers, an infantry regiment of "galvanized" Confederate prisoners of war who had agreed to serve in the West instead of being held in Federal camps. The raid began on July 26 with an attack on a wagon train bringing supplies to the post with a 23-man escort. A small party sent out from the post to reinforce the wagon train was ambushed, and one officer and four men were killed. Even so, the firepower of the wagon train, which included a mountain howitzer as well as the carbines of the troops and wagoners, was enough to drive back the attackers. The Indians broke off the raid, which had been designed to cut one of the major telegraph lines and immigration routes to the west. Its failure also caused the break-up of the tribal confederation that had been created for the effort.

Below: It was standard cavalry practice at the beginning of a skirmish in the Indian wars for the men to dismount and take up positions behind cover as a few men, still mounted, moved the troop's horses to the rear.

Washakie, chief of the Shoshoni in Wyoming helped the whites fight other western tribes.

The Powder River Expedition

Connor did not believe that hostilities would end there. In July, he led his column, including men of the 2nd California, 15th and 16th Kansas, 6th Michigan, 12th Missouri, and 7th and 11th Ohio Cavalry, along the Powder River. On August 29, the column drove 300 warriors and the other inhabitants out of an Arapaho village and burned it, and then pressed ahead. Their advance was now facing limited Indian opposition, but there were serious threats from cold weather, exhaustion, and shortages of food. On September 5, the column drove off an Indian attack, but was engulfed in a dreadful storm that killed 514 horses and mules during a single night. The column pulled back to Fort Connor, which had been built just before the departure of this ill-advised expedition and Connor abandoned all hopes of further effort during that frustrating year and departed to Salt Lake City. The same lack of overall success affected Sully's column of Dakota, Iowa, and Minnesota cavalrymen, who moved around their allotted area in June and July. On July 28, the garrison of Fort Rice drove off a Sioux attack after a three-hour fight, but even though Sully set off in pursuit, he was unable to catch the retreating war party.

The 1865 campaign was therefore a failure. The task was then gradually reassumed by regular units arriving from the east after the Civil War, but the last volunteer units on the Indian frontier, including the 11th Ohio Cavalry, were not disbanded until July 12, 1866. The regular army moved back into the system of regional defense that had been established in the 1850s. It still seemed valid, despite the mixed fortunes of the volunteer units that had manned the frontier in the first half of the 1860s. In the second half of 1866, the command and administrative structure for frontier defense included the Division of the Missouri with its subordinate Departments of Arkansas, Dakota, Missouri, and the Platte, the Division of the Pacific with its subordinate Departments of California and the Columbia, and the independent Department of the Gulf, which included Texas. As the U.S. presence in the west increased, this organization was later modified to suit new operational and administrative needs.

More Cavalry Is Raised

The summer of 1866 was comparatively peaceful along the tribal frontier, and there was time to replace volunteers with regulars. The superiority of cavalry over infantry in Indian fighting had been fully confirmed during the period when volunteer units held the frontier, and the regular army was now given more horse power. Six cavalry regiments emerged from the Civil War, and on July 28, 1866, Congress authorized another four cavalry regiments. They were created on September 21 and included the 7th Cavalry at Fort Riley, Kansas; the 8th Cavalry at Angel Island, California; the 9th Cavalry at Greenville, Louisiana; and the 10th Cavalry at Fort Leavenworth. Like the first six regiments, the 7th and 8th Cavalry were white regiments, while the 9th and 10th Cavalry had black troopers and white officers.

The comparative quiet in the summer of 1866 also allowed the army a period of grace to assess its position along the Indian frontier, where the foe was the hostile environment as much as the

Chief Trumpeter, 1st Cavalry Regiment, U.S. Army, 1873.

This important noncommissioned officer is seen in dress uniform, which includes the musician's dress coat adorned with a streamlined herringbone lace arrangement. Chevrons of the pattern shown here were authorized on June 25, 1873. Lower on the sleeve are two diagonal markings: the red stripe indicates service in the Civil War, and the gold stripe five years of service.

Brigadier General Edward Richard Sprigg Canby, a Civil War veteran who was murdered by the Modoc Indians in 1873 while attempting to negotiate with them.

Below:
Major General Neilson Appleton Miles and "Buffalo Bill" Cody survey the camp of hostile Sioux Indians near the Pine Ridge Agency, South Dakota, on January 16, 1891.

Indian. General Grant sent a number of officers to the frontier to observe and report on conditions of all types. The overall assessment showed Grant and his staff that the area was either uninhabited or at best very thinly populated, and that the huge size of the region, combined with extremes of terrain and climate, aggravated the army's overall manpower shortages, logistical limitations, communications difficulties, and movement problems even where the slow extension of railroad lines was improving matters.

The most important factor brought to Grant's attention, though, was the different nature and capabilities of the "cavalry" Indian of the Great Plains compared with the "infantry" tribes that the army had fought in its earlier campaigns east of the Mississippi River. The army had understood this fact in the ten years before the Civil War, but the direct experience of the men and officers of the period had been largely

lost during the Civil War.

Few of the officers who rose to positions of command immediately after the Civil War had any previous experience with the Plains Indians. Grant himself, for example, had left the army in 1854 because of a drinking problem caused mainly by the loneliness of life in a frontier outpost where nothing ever happened. Sherman had no western experience whatsoever; Sheridan had limited experience as a junior officer in the northwest for five years; and both Brigadier General O. Howard and Colonel N. Miles, like Sherman, lacked any frontier experience. Other men who rose to prominence on the Indian frontier, such as George Armstrong Custer, Ranald Slidell Mackenzie, and Wesley Merritt, had all graduated from West Point during the Civil War. On the other side of the tactical coin, a number of experienced commanders were lost to the service: Sully faded into the obscurity of regimental command, Cooke

Above: Major General Miles with his staff. Miles had a distinguished record in the Civil War, reaching the rank of major general in the U.S. Volunteers. He played a major part in the Indian wars and was promoted to brigadier general in 1860 and to major general in 1890. From 1895 he was commanding general of the army and was promoted to lieutenant general in 1900, three years before his retirement.

Left: Known to the Indians he fought as ''Gray Fox,'' Major General George Crook was the army's most successful Indian fighter. Crook is seen here with his riding mule, and two Apache scouts known as ''Dutchy'' and ''Alchiss.''

43

Still one of the most controversial American leaders of his period, George Armstrong Custer is seen in the uniform of a major general, the rank in the U.S. Volunteers which he reached on April 15, 1865, at the age of 25. Between the 1st Battle of Bull Run and Lee's surrender at Appomattox Court House, Custer took part in all but one of the Army of the Potomac's battles. He had 11 horses killed under him, but suffered only one wound. Continuing in the regular army after the war as colonel of the 7th Cavalry Regiment, Custer was killed at the Battle of the Little Big Horn together with his brother, Thomas Ward Custer, who served as his aide.

retired in 1873, and Edward Richard Sprigg Canby was murdered by Modoc Indians in 1873. The only senior officer with previous frontier experience was Major General George Crook, and it is perhaps no surprise, therefore, that he became the best Indian-fighting general that the U.S. Army ever had.

Most of the officers who came to the Indian frontier had learned the practical aspects of their profession against the Confederacy. Many of these officers had outstanding records and reputations, but only those who approached their new situation with an open mind became effective Indian fighters and, in some

George Custer
For further references see pages
43, 46, 51, 52, *59*, *61*, 64, 65, 67, 70, 72, 73, 87, *92*,

George Crook
For further references see pages
43, 62, 63, 64, 67, 92, 93, 116, 117, 120, *121*, 124

cases, decisive instruments in solving the Indian problem.

Gold: Another Cause of Friction

Even as the Civil War was raging in the east, another cause for conflict was raising its head in the west; as gold was discovered in Montana. Inevitably, prospectors and miners headed for the goldfields around Virginia City, and most of them complained about the difficulty of access to the area. The army replied with a survey of more direct routes, and finally chose for the one pioneered by John Bozeman. This trail left the Oregon Trail at Fort Laramie on the North Platte River and moved northwest along the eastern side of the Bighorn Mountains and around their northern shoulder. In terms of terrain it was a good trail, but it crossed the hunting grounds that had been reserved for the Sioux, Northern Cheyennes, and Arapahoes in an 1865 treaty. The tribes resisted movement along the Bozeman Trail; Connor's Powder River expedition, which had achieved so little, was an effort to secure this route.

Public pressure was exerted on the government in Washington, which was also attracted by the prospect of gold to ease national finances straitened by the Civil War. New negotiations were opened with the Indians, and some tribes reached an accommodation with Washington in a treaty signed at Fort Laramie. However, Chief Red Cloud of the Oglala Sioux and other Indian leaders refused to consider any modification of the 1865 treaty. They walked out of the negotiations when news arrived that Colonel Henry Beebe Carrington and a battalion of the 18th Infantry had marched into the hunting grounds to build posts along the Bozeman Trail, which was to be turned into a wagon road.

Red Cloud's War

Carrington and his 700 men departed from Fort Laramie in June 1866 and headed for Bighorn country. Red Cloud had announced that any incursion would be met by force, yet the battalion was

accompanied by many families, including Carrington's. Two companies of the 5th Volunteers (another unit of "galvanized" Confederates) were relieved at Fort Reno by a regular company, and Carrington pushed on northwest to build his headquarters post, Fort Phil Kearny, 225 miles from Fort Laramie on the Piney River, a tributary of the Powder River. Five companies were detached to garrison Fort Phil Kearny, and the last two were sent forward another 90 miles to build Fort C.F. Smith on the northern edge of the Bighorn Mountains.

As the main bastion of U.S. strength on the Bozeman Trail, Fort Kearny was inevitably the focus of Indian attack, and during the fort's brief life, it was under virtually constant Indian siege. On December 21, 1866, a wood-gathering party was attacked about six miles from the fort, and Captain William J. Fetterman received permission to lead a relief force. Fetterman, who had been brevetted lieutenant colonel in the Civil War, boasted that he could ride through

In 1866, the government bought more than 15 million acres of land from the Creek, Seminole, Choctaw, and Chickasaw Indians, with the intention of providing homesteading land for freedmen. In May 1879, a homesteading "race," advertised in the poster shown above, was open for all people eager to claim their 160 free acres in Independence, Kansas.

the entire Sioux nation with just 80 men. He and his 80-man detachment were decoyed over Lodge Trail Ridge, too far from the fort for any possibility of quick retreat or even reinforcement. They paid with the lives of all whites present, including two civilians who were evaluating Henry repeating rifles, the Springfield muzzleloaders of the 18th Infantry and the Spencer breech-loaders of the 2nd Cavalry. Attacked by 2,000 Sioux under Chief Crazy Horse, Fetterman's detachment survived for only 40 minutes; in that time, they managed to kill 60 Sioux and wound another 300.

There was great public outrage at this "Fetterman Massacre," and Major General Winfield Scott Hancock was ordered to pursue and destroy Crazy Horse's band with Lieutenant Colonel George A. Custer's 7th Cavalry plus supporting infantry and artillery. On April 19, 1867, the cavalry found and burned 111 Cheyenne and 140 Sioux lodges at Pawnee Creek. Custer then showed poor judgment; he ordered his exhausted men to push forward on equally exhausted horses. Custer eventually rejoined Hancock, who decided that defensive attack was needed.

The Hayfield and Wagon Box Fights

Hancock's decision was unadventurous but probably right, for it resulted in two engagements in which the superior firepower and discipline of the American soldiers prevailed. The first was the "Hayfield Fight" near Fort C.F. Smith on August 1. A haymaking detail of 19 soldiers and six civilians, commanded by Lieutenant Sigismund Sternberg and equipped with Springfield rifles converted to breech-loading, held back a far larger force of Indians with the loss of only three men killed and another three wounded. The second, and more important, engagement was the "Wagon Box Fight" near Fort Phil Kearny on August 2. A wood-gathering detail of 31 men under Captain

Plains Indians attack a stagecoach of the Butterfield Overland Dispatch service in 1866.

Cheyenne warrior, 1876.

This warrior wears clothing typical of the Indians of the Great Plains; his weapons are the bow (with arrows carried in the quiver on the warrior's back) and a knife. The white stripes painted on the warrior's face indicated that members of his family had been killed by white men, and that he would avenge their deaths.

James Powell was surrounded by 1,000 or more Indians. Powell ordered his men to improvise defenses out of wagon beds taken off their wheels. With their breech-loading Springfield conversions, they held off repeated mounted and foot attacks for four hours, with only three killed and two wounded.

The Indians suffered heavy losses in these two fights, but the army lacked the strength to mount offensive operations that might have capitalized on these reverses. Red Cloud was an able diplomat, however, and realized that there was a swell of opinion in the east for negotiation rather than war. In 1868, Red Cloud signed a treaty with Washington, and the army abandoned the Bozeman Trail and the posts along it. The Indians celebrated the end of the only war they won against the U.S. Army by burning down Fort Phil Kearny.

Throughout the period of the Indian wars, the army was never able to match its available skills and supplies with the demands made on these resources. The two reasons were lack of adequate resources and poor communications in an operational theater of vast size. The commander of the Division of the Missouri, Lieutenant General Sherman, said: "Were I or the department commanders to send guards to every point where they are clamored for, we would need alone on the plains a hundred thousand men, mostly of cavalry. Each spot of every road, and each little settlement along five thousand miles of frontier, wants its regiment of cavalry or infantry to protect it against the combined power of all the Indians, because of the bare possibility of their being attacked by the combined force of all the Indians."

Fortunately for the settlers and the army, the Indians were seldom able to decide and implement a concerted plan within each tribe, let alone between tribes, so large-scale threats seldom developed. The tribal way of life and war dictated spasmodic and unconcerted action along long stretches of the frontier, and the only way that the army could react rapidly was to locate its resources in comparatively small detachments at strategic points on and behind the frontier.

Forsyth's Scout Force

Even so, troops and units were in short supply. In an effort to provide an alternative, the commander of the Department of the Missouri, Major General P. Sheridan, in 1868 ordered Major George Alexander Forsyth to "employ fifty first-class hardy frontiersmen, to be used as scouts against the hostile Indians, to be commanded by yourself." Forsyth recruited these men at Forts Harker and Hays in Kansas, and late in August, he led his men into an area known to be used by the Arapaho, Comanche, Kiowa, and Southern Cheyenne as well as Sioux south of their normal range·along the Platte River.

The area was full of unrest, for the Kansas Pacific Railroad was being pushed through the region. Buffalo were being killed to feed railroad workers and otherwise frightened away, while eastern settlers were beginning to arrive in the districts opened up by the railroad. The Cheyenne also remembered the Sand

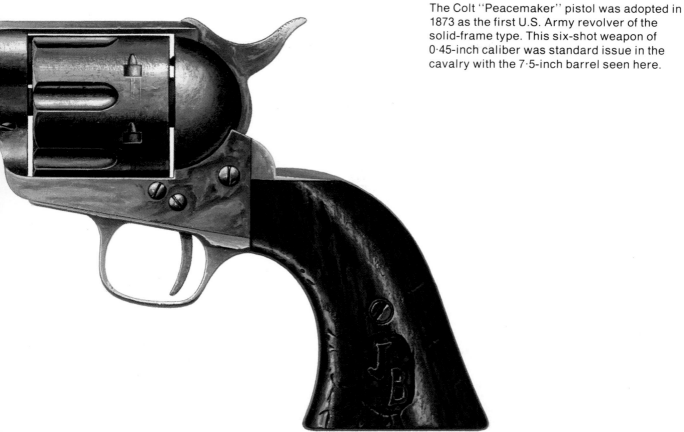

The Colt "Peacemaker" pistol was adopted in 1873 as the first U.S. Army revolver of the solid-frame type. This six-shot weapon of 0·45-inch caliber was standard issue in the cavalry with the 7·5-inch barrel seen here.

Creek Massacre, a fact they had made abundantly clear to Hancock's expedition through the region in the previous year.

The Battle of Beecher's Island

The inevitable collision took place on September 17, 1868. Forsyth's little command encountered a war party of 600 Arapaho, Cheyenne, and Sioux on the Arickaree Fork of the Republican River in the extreme east of Colorado. In what became known as the Battle of Beecher's Island, the Indians besieged Forsyth's command on a small island, a sandbar in the sluggish stream, for three days. Army casualties were five dead and more than 20 wounded, the former including Lieutenant Frederick H. Beecher, Forsyth's second in command, and the latter Forsyth himself. The Indians lost only nine dead, but one of them was the great war chief Bat, known to the Americans as Roman Nose. The death of Roman Nose deterred the Indians from

launching any more direct attacks, but they maintained their siege of the island until September 25, when Forsyth's command was reached by a detachment of the 10th Cavalry under Captain Louis H. Carpenter.

By this time, the authorities in Washington had abandoned their policy of forcibly removing tribes from areas wanted by white settlers. (The most notable of these enforced relocations had been that of the Five Civilized Tribes from the southeast to Oklahoma along the "Trail of Tears," as it was called by the Cherokees.) Instead, the government decided to concentrate the Indians in designated areas called reservations. Such a policy had many theoretical and logistical attractions, but in practice it forced many tribes from their ancestral lands into areas that were often little more than desert, and sometimes placed completely incompatible tribes on the same reservation. Some tribes accepted the practice. Others remained on the reservation only during the winter so that

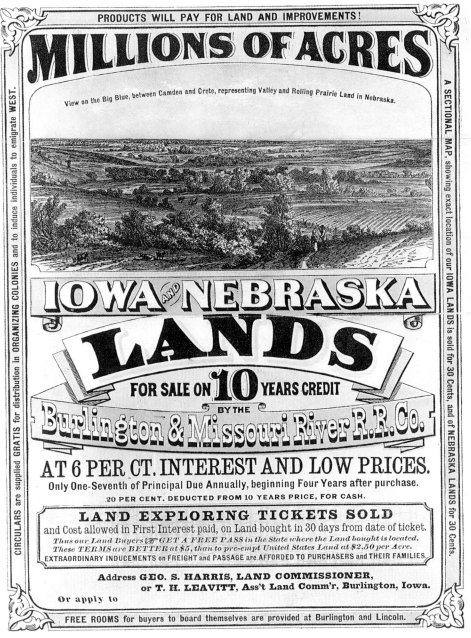

PRODUCTS WILL PAY FOR LAND AND IMPROVEMENTS!

MILLIONS OF ACRES

View on the Big Blue, between Camden and Crete, representing Valley and Rolling Prairie Land in Nebraska.

IOWA AND NEBRASKA LANDS

FOR SALE ON **10** YEARS CREDIT

BY THE

Burlington & Missouri River R.R. Co.

AT 6 PER CT. INTEREST AND LOW PRICES.

Only One-Seventh of Principal Due Annually, beginning Four Years after purchase.

20 PER CENT. DEDUCTED FROM 10 YEARS PRICE, FOR CASH.

LAND EXPLORING TICKETS SOLD

and Cost allowed in First Interest paid, on Land bought in 30 days from date of ticket.

Thus our Land Buyers ☞ GET A FREE PASS in the State where the Land bought is located. These TERMS are BETTER at $5, than to pre-empt United States Land at $2.50 per Acre.

EXTRAORDINARY INDUCEMENTS on FREIGHT and PASSAGE are AFFORDED TO PURCHASERS and THEIR FAMILIES.

Address **GEO. S. HARRIS, LAND COMMISSIONER,**
or **T. H. LEAVITT, Ass't Land Comm'r, Burlington, Iowa.**

Or apply to

FREE ROOMS for buyers to board themselves are provided at Burlington and Lincoln.

CIRCULARS are supplied GRATIS for distribution in ORGANIZING COLONIES and to induce individuals to emigrate WEST.

A SECTIONAL MAP, showing exact location of our IOWA LANDS is sold for 30 Cents, and of NEBRASKA LANDS for 30 Cents.

Continued movement of settlers to the west, a source of constant friction with the native Americans already in the affected areas, was encouraged by a succession of promotions such as that advertised in this circular that helped create the Oklahoma land rush.

they could receive government rations before departing to hunt or raid during the summer. Still others refused even to consider the practice or to limit themselves to specific geographical areas.

Sheridan plans the Washita Campaign

The army had to implement government policy, and Sheridan decided that a winter campaign would produce the best results. An astute commander, he knew that the type of operation he envisaged presented many problems, especially logistical ones, but he also appreciated that it offered the chance for decisive results since the mobility of the Indians would be limited. Sheridan calculated correctly that the Indians' winter encampments, limited food supplies, and thin ponies were a prime target. They could not be moved easily or swiftly, and their destruction or capture would leave the Indians, both warriors and their dependents, with the choice of facing the elements or surrendering to the army.

Sheridan planned, in short, a total war, like his Shenandoah Valley campaign, but adapted to fit the tactical nature of warfare against the Indians.

Sheridan's plan called for three forces to converge and hit the Indian winter grounds between the Canadian and Washita rivers just east of the Texas Panhandle. One force was to advance southeast from Fort Lyon, Colorado, under Major General Eugene Asa Carr. Another was to move east from Fort Bascom, New Mexico, under Colonel Evans, and the last was to push south from Fort Dodge, Kansas, under Sully. Carr's force left Fort Lyon on December 2, 1868, and eventually established a base camp on the upper reaches of the Canadian River just west of a similar camp set up by Evans's force, which had left Fort Bascom on November 18. The main force left Fort Dodge on November 12 and built Camp Supply on the North Canadian River from November 18. Three days later, Sheridan arrived and replaced Sully with Custer.

The Battle of Washita River

Custer led 800 men of his 7th Cavalry from Camp Supply under the cover of a blizzard on November 23. The 7th Cavalry crossed the Canadian River, and four days after leaving camp, they found about 75 lodges on the upper reaches of the Washita River. This camp was the winter home of a band of the generally peaceful Southern Cheyennes under Chief Black Kettle. With the army band playing "Garry Owen," the regimental march, Custer launched his attack before undertaking even the most rudimentary reconnaissance. The 11 companies attacked at dawn in three groups from the north, the northwest and the southwest. The result was a confused melee known as the Battle of Washita River, though it was more a massacre than a real battle. The Cheyennes fought back as best they could, killing six of Custer's men and wounding several more, but they lost 105 dead including Black Kettle, 38 warriors, and 66 women. However, army casualties were increased by the deaths of Major Joel Elliott and 19 troopers. They were ambushed well within earshot of the main force, and rescue by Custer should have been simple.

By mid-morning, Custer had discovered what reconnaissance would have told him at an earlier time: that Black Kettle's village was just one of several Arapaho, Cheyenne, and Kiowa settlements in the area. The scene was later described by Major E.S. Godfrey: "he was

This contemporary illustration depicts a desperate engagement between the Cheyennes and Company G, 7th Cavalry Regiment, near Fort Wallace, Kansas, on June 26, 1867. Such small-scale actions were typical of the wars between the U.S. Army and the Indian tribes of the Great Plains.

ordered, after charging through the village, to take my platoon and bring in the pony herd. While executing this I saw some dismounted Indians escaping over the hills on the opposite side of the creek. I sent the herd in by a guard, and made a pursuit. The Indians picked up a herd out grazing, mounted and made escape. I followed for nearly four miles, until I saw in the open valley beyond them a large village. The escaping Indians began circling, and the warriors started to their rescue. Retreat was necessary."

Custer learned that these fresh warriors were hastening from the other villages to tackle the U.S. cavalry, and that departure might be difficult. The 7th Cavalry burned Black Kettle's village, shot 700 Indian ponies, and after an offensive feint toward the arriving warriors, pulled back with 53 women and children as captives.

The Battle of the Washita made Custer famous with the American public as a fearless and effective Indian fighter. It made his name with the Indians in an altogether different way, one which was to have dire consequences in the future.

Colonel Evans later led his 3rd Cavalry forward from its base camp on the Canadian River and struck a Kiowa encampment at Soldier Spring on December 25. Like Custer's effort on the Washita River, it was a severe physical as well as psychological blow to the Indians of the southern plains.

Custer was still full of fight after his return to Camp Supply on December 2, and five days later set out once more with Sheridan for Fort Cobb. From there, the 7th Cavalry swung south to Fort Sill. Custer headed out from Fort Sill on March 2, 1869, west to the Salt Fork of the Red River. Turning northeast, he reached a Cheyenne camp on Sweetwater Creek about 25 miles west of his triumph at the Washita River. He talked the Cheyennes into surrender on March 18, in the process securing the release of two women settlers who had been captured by the Cheyenne.

In June, 1869, the 5th Cavalry departed from Fort McPherson on the Platte River on another search and destroy operation.

General William Tecumseh Sherman and the American commissioners in council with Indian chiefs at Fort Laramie in 1867 or 1868.

Officer, 7th Cavalry Regiment, U.S. Army, 1876.

This officer wears the stylish, but only semi-official, dress favored by regiments in field service in frontier regions, including the so-called "fireman's shirt" and buckskin pants. Officers of the 7th Cavalry wore crossed sabers with the regimental number embroidered in yellow or white silk on the corners of their shirt collars. In general, emphasis was placed on practicality rather than uniformity in strict accordance with the dress regulations. This officer wears a cartridge belt carrying ammunition for his Springfield carbine around his waist.

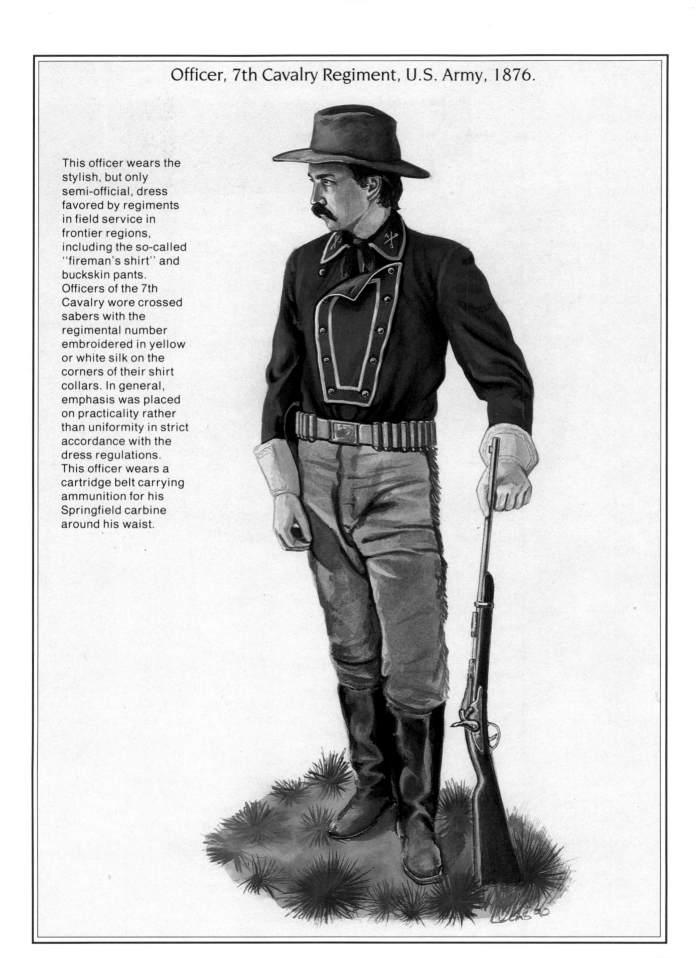

While waiting for the level of the South Platte River to fall enough for its horses to cross, the cavalry found a Pawnee village. An immediate attack was launched to destroy this settlement, and in the fighting one woman settler was rescued, though another was killed. The cavalry continued its operations through the summer of 1869 in a campaign that finally ended the resistance of the Cheyenne and their allies in the Republican and Smoky Hills.

All wars have a moral dimension, sometimes small but often large. The moral dimension entered strongly into the Indian wars with Sheridan's introduction of the idea of total war. This concept had troubled a number of his own soldiers, but their disquiet was pushed into the background when the outright military efficiency of the policy revealed itself in declining Indian resistance. The moral dimension had a stronger influence on the civilian population of the east, however, and its impact peaked early in 1870.

On January 23, two squadrons of the 2nd Cavalry attacked and destroyed a Piegan village on the Marias River in Montana. Eastern newspaper reports of the incident did much to polarize public opinion against Sheridan's tactical thinking. As a result, government policy switched increasingly to a search for peaceful solutions to the Indian problem.

Despite the conciliatory moves inaugurated by this revised government policy, the Cheyenne and Kiowa were still basically unwilling to yield their traditional hunting grounds and abandon the way of life that went with them. Some of the tribes did settle restlessly on the reservation around Fort Sill in the Indian Territory, but others continued to hold out.

Sherman Becomes Commanding General

Sherman was now commanding general of the U.S. Army, and his previous position at the head of the Division of the Missouri had been assumed by Sheridan with the rank of lieutenant general. Both these senior commanders realized that continued campaigning was needed to keep the problem of the Plains Indians under control. In 1871, for example, a party of Kiowa left the reservation and raided into Texas, where they killed some of the teamsters on a government wagon train at Salt Creek Prairie on May 18, 1871, before returning to the reservation. One of the raiders boasted of his courage in front of the reservation agent, a Quaker who reported the information to Colonel Benjamin Henry Grierson, commanding the 10th Cavalry.

Sherman was on a visit to Fort Sill at the time and had coordinated the original, unsuccessful search for the perpetrators. Now the army's commanding general arrested the three leaders of the raid (Satanta, Satank, and Lone Tree) in

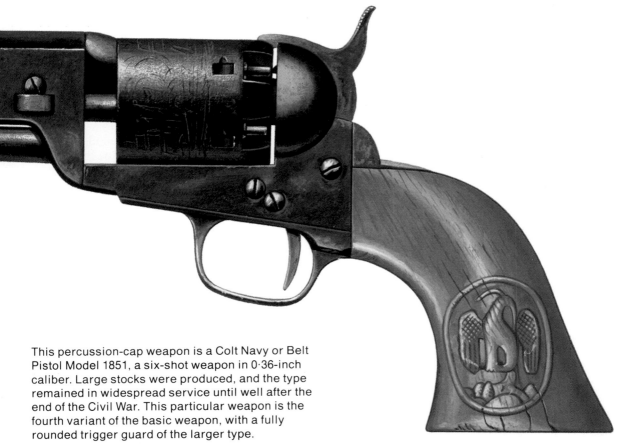

This percussion-cap weapon is a Colt Navy or Belt Pistol Model 1851, a six-shot weapon in 0·36-inch caliber. Large stocks were produced, and the type remained in widespread service until well after the end of the Civil War. This particular weapon is the fourth variant of the basic weapon, with a fully rounded trigger guard of the larger type.

an extraordinary confrontation between armed Indians and U.S. soldiers. The situation was extremely volatile, and only Sherman's cool presence kept the lid on matters. Satank was killed as he tried to escape from custody on the way to his trial, and the other two men were convicted and sentenced to death. Political pressure guaranteed that the sentences were commuted to life imprisonment, and both men were released on parole after only two years in prison. Sherman was furious, and his anger was fully vindicated when Satanta again went raiding and killing.

By the 1870s, the Indian problem on the southern plains had been reduced, but was by no means over. In 1871, the 6th Cavalry was replaced in Texas by the 4th Cavalry, which had been trained by Colonel Mackenzie into what many considered the finest cavalry regiment in the army. In the fall of 1871, the 4th Cavalry skirmished frequently with the Comanches on the Staked Plains and returned to the same task in 1872. The cavalry's greatest success that year

came on September 29, when the troops surprised Chief Mow-way's band of Kot-soteka Comanches on the North Fork of the Red River, decisively beating them before burning their village. Even so, the Cheyenne, Comanche, and Kiowa were not unduly disturbed and rebuilt their confidence in 1873. During the following winter, they frequently raided into northern Texas.

The Red River War

The result was the Red River War. On July 20, 1874, Sherman ordered Sheridan to wage a ruthless campaign against the troublesome tribes. Sheridan's plan called for a triple advance by some 3,000 soldiers under the tactical command of Colonel Nelson Miles against the tribes in the Texas Panhandle. The 6th Cavalry and Miles's 5th Infantry were to drive south from Fort Dodge, Kansas, the 8th Cavalry was to move east down the Canadian River, the 10th Cavalry was to push west from Fort Sill, and the 4th Cavalry and

10th Infantry were to advance north.

Launched in the summer, the offensive force faced not only the Indians, but also temperatures that climbed as high as 110°, an acute shortage of water, and lack of grass for the horses after a plague of locusts had cleared the region. These difficulties notwithstanding, the offensive secured valuable successes. The 6th Cavalry destroyed several Indian villages on the Staked Plains Escarpment, while the 8th Cavalry located, chased, and dispersed large numbers of Indians.

The Battle of Palo Duro Canyon

The 4th Cavalry, supported by four companies of the 10th Infantry, was attacked by a large war party, but drove it off. The following day, Sergeant Charlton and a scouting party trailed the retreating Indians, and suddenly found themselves above a deep canyon. At the bottom of Palo Duro Canyon was the camp the Indians were establishing as the winter base for the Arapaho, Cheyenne, Comanche, and Kiowa. Charlton galloped the 25 miles back to Mackenzie's main body and reported the discovery. By dawn on September 27, the 4th Cavalry and its accompanying infantry were in position on the rim of the canyon. The only way down was a narrow and slippery goat path, and the cavalrymen led their nervous horses down this path like a long blue snake. The snake's head had almost reached the floor of the canyon before a warrior realized the situation and raised the alarm.

Responding with their customary speed, the Kiowa moved straight into the attack. It was the right tactic, as the cavalry arriving at the bottom of the path were disorganized, but Mackenzie had foreseen the situation and posted sharpshooters on a ledge from which they could fire into any Indian advance. The Indians hesitated as their leading men were shot down. This pause bought the cavalry just enough time for them to form up and charge. The first troop soon returned with a herd of captured ponies. By this time, two more troops had reached the floor of the canyon, and they now charged the retreating Kiowa. With Mackenzie at their head, these two troops pursued the Kiowa for five miles along the canyon floor before turning back in the face of increasing Indian fire from the canyon walls.

Mackenzie ordered the captured ponies to be herded up onto the open plain, where they were shot so there would be no chance of their later escape and recapture by the Indians. The Americans then pulled back after burning the village and its food stocks. The only American casualty was a trumpeter who was shot in the stomach but made a full recovery.

The Battle of Palo Duro Canyon was a decisive blow against the Kiowa, who were left without horses and now faced the prospect of the typically harsh winter without adequate stocks of food. Soon the weather began to deteriorate, and faced with rain, hail, and wind storms, the soldiers and troopers pulled back to their bases. There was no such option for the Indians. Most moved to reservations, though some of the Southern Cheyenne managed to reach the Northern Cheyenne. Satanta surrendered on October 24, 1874, and was immediately shipped back to prison. Despairing of release, he committed suicide in 1876 by jumping out of a window. By March, 1875, most of the Indians of the southern plains had surrendered to the army.

The last act of the Red River War came on April 23, 1875, at Sappa Creek, Kansas. Here, a troop of the 6th Cavalry caught a band of 60 Indians. In a short engagement, the cavalry lost two men killed, but captured more than half of the Indians.

The German Incident

This period was also marked by one of those episodes that appear in history with an odd frequency, even though they appear to be the stuff of fiction rather than fact. On September 9, 1874, an emigrant family named German was intercepted by a band of Cheyenne traveling through Kansas. The Indians killed the father, mother, and son of the family, and scalped the one of five daughters who had long hair. The other four daughters were carried off, the two older girls by one band and the two younger girls (aged ten and five) by another band led by Chief Gray Beard.

When Miles heard of the incident, he ordered all troops under his command to search for the surviving girls. Even detachments on other tasks were ordered to keep their eyes open. One, a troop of cavalry and a company of the 5th Infantry under Lieutenant Frank D. Baldwin, was escorting a train of 25 empty wagons on its return to a supply depot. On November 8, 1874, scouts informed Baldwin, whose detachment was camped near McClellan's Creek, Texas, that there was a large party of Indians in the area, and that one of the tepees appeared to be that of Gray Beard. Baldwin, already the recipient of a Medal of Honor in the Civil War, decided on a surprise attack in very unusual fashion. Stationing his cavalry on the flanks, he arranged the wagons in a double column. One wagon contained a mountain howitzer, and the others each contained a squad of infantry. The combined force of cavalry and wagon-mounted infantry moved quietly to the ridge line above the Indian camp and then charged to the sound of cavalry bugle and infantry trumpet.

The startled Cheyennes bolted from their tepees to be greeted by rifle fire from the infantry and pistol fire from the cavalry. The first charge swept through the Indian camp, followed by a series of other charges over a period of four hours. Baldwin's command drove the Indians 15 miles from their camp and dispersed them. Only at this point did Baldwin recall his command and head back to the camp. There, the Americans found the two German girls, who were hungry, bruised, and ragged, but otherwise unharmed. For his courage and determination, Baldwin was

Tales of white women and children taken prisoner by Indians always aroused enormous interest in the press. An earlier "version" of the German family episode was that of the Oatman family. Here, Olive Oatman arrives at Fort Yuma, Arizona, in 1855, after being held captive for nearly five years by Apache and Mojave Indians who had massacred the rest of the Oatman family.

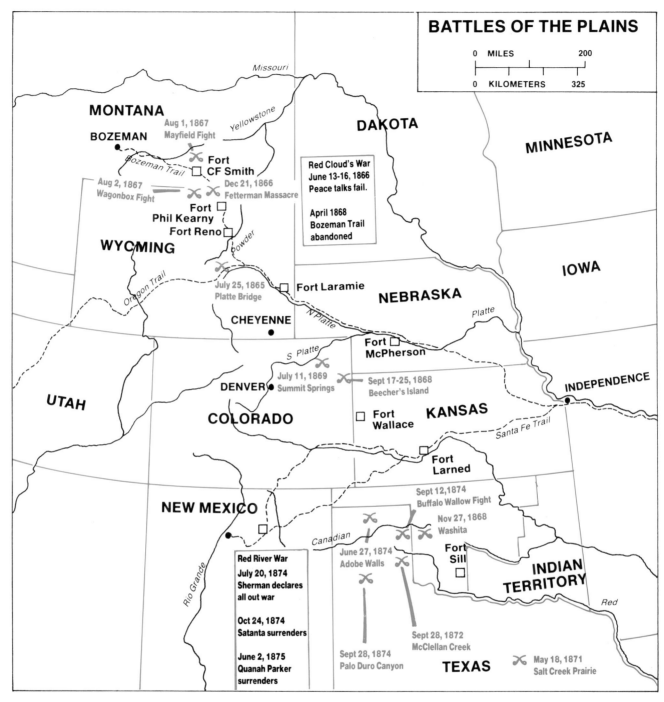

BATTLES OF THE PLAINS

0 MILES 200

0 KILOMETERS 325

Missouri

MONTANA

BOZEMAN

Aug 1, 1867
Mayfield Fight

Yellowstone

Bozeman Trail

Fort
CF Smith

DAKOTA

MINNESOTA

Aug 2, 1867
Wagonbox Fight

Dec 21, 1866
Fetterman Massacre

Red Cloud's War
June 13-16, 1866
Peace talks fail.

April 1868
Bozeman Trail
abandoned

Fort
Phil Kearny

Fort Reno

Powder

WYOMING

Oregon Trail

July 25, 1865
Platte Bridge

Fort Laramie

NEBRASKA

N Platte

IOWA

Platte

CHEYENNE

S Platte

Fort
McPherson

July 11, 1869
Summit Springs

Sept 17-25, 1868
Beecher's Island

INDEPENDENCE

UTAH

DENVER

COLORADO

Fort
Wallace

KANSAS

Santa Fe Trail

Fort
Larned

Sept 12, 1874
Buffalo Wallow Fight

NEW MEXICO

Canadian

Nov 27, 1868
Washita

June 27, 1874
Adobe Walls

Fort
Sill

INDIAN
TERRITORY

Rio Grande

Red River War

July 20, 1874
Sherman declares
all out war

Oct 24, 1874
Satanta surrenders

June 2, 1875
Quanah Parker
surrenders

Sept 28, 1874
Palo Duro Canyon

Sept 28, 1872
McClellan Creek

TEXAS

Red

May 18, 1871
Salt Creek Prairie

awarded a second Medal of Honor.

Miles soon closed in and compelled the Cheyenne to release the two older German girls. The sisters were able to identify 75 of the warriors involved in the murder of the rest of their family, who were sent to prison in Florida. The sisters recovered from their ordeal and were supported until they married by funds diverted at Miles' insistence from govern-

ment subsidies for the Indians.

The Red River War effectively ended the resistance of the Indian tribes on the southern plains, the tribes remained on their reservations in the Indian Territory (later Oklahoma), Kansas, and Texas. The army was free to divert some of its precious resources to other areas, where there was still continued trouble.

On the northern plains, raids by

Battles of the campaigns on the great plains.

Another feature of the Indian wars guaranteed to attract the interest of Americans was the massacre of settlers by the Indians. Taken from his 1874 book, *My Life on the Plains*, this shows Colonel George Custer at the scene of the Kidder massacre.

the Northern Cheyenne and Sioux throughout the winter of 1873-74 were just part of the problem with these tribes that had continued since the end of Red Cloud's War. The treaty that ended this war in 1868 had set aside the Great Sioux Reservation west of the Missouri River in southern Dakota for exclusive Indian use. There were also large numbers of Indians in the disputed lands along the Powder River in Wyoming and Montana. The Northern Cheyenne and Sioux were located in considerable numbers just north of the Platte River, one of the major transcontinental routes used by westbound migrants. The situation was fraught with danger, but the arrangement was workable as long as there was no reason for Americans to intrude on Indian lands. However the development of American civilization meant that encroachment was inevitable.

For several years, the Indians refused to allow a right of way through their lands

for the Northern Pacific Railroad. Even so, the railroad company refused to admit defeat and sent surveyors into the areas through which it wished to push its tracks. The survey parties were resisted by the Indians, the railroad appealed to the government for protection, and in 1873, Colonel David Sloan Stanley led a military expedition into the Yellowstone valley.

The following year, Sheridan ordered Custer to undertake a reconnaissance of the Black Hills, an area well within the Great Sioux Reservation. Custer left Fort Abraham Lincoln on July 10, 1874, with ten companies of the 7th Cavalry and two companies of infantry, and pushed into the Black Hills. There were geologists with Custer's force, and they discovered gold in the Black Hills. The news soon leaked out, and despite the army's efforts, prospectors began to trickle into the area in steadily increasing numbers. The Indians of the reservation were angry that the Americans had broken yet another

The growing network of railroads were a constant source of anger to the Indians of the Great Plains. Here, they attack a group of workers on a hand-car of the Pacific Railroad in a running fight that saw the repulse of the Indians.

treaty, and they began drifting west into the Powder River area in large numbers. There, they linked up with Indians who had never subscribed to the 1868 treaty. The situation became increasingly volatile.

The Sioux War of 1876

In December, 1875, the Indian Bureau told the Northern Cheyenne and Sioux in the Powder River area that they must move onto the reservation by the end of January, 1876. Even if the Indians had been willing to heed these orders, it would have been impossible for them to make such a move from winter quarters in a remote area during the dead of winter. The deadline passed, and the Commissioner of Indian Affairs appealed to the army to force the Indians to move. Sheridan agreed and, remembering the success of his tactic of converging columns on the southern plains, he decided to use the same system again.

In the bitterly cold weather of March,

1876, and as a preliminary to the main offensive planned for the summer, ten companies of cavalry from Crook's column, under the command of Colonel Joseph Jones Reynolds, advanced into the upper end of the Powder River valley and surprised the winter quarters of Chief Crazy Horse of the Oglala Sioux. In the Battle of Slim Buttes on March 17, 800 troopers destroyed the encampment, but Reynolds was unable to press his initial advantage when a frightened subordinate ordered a withdrawal. This gave the Sioux the chance to regroup, whereupon they counterattacked with such vehemence that Reynolds fell back toward Crook's main force. Sheridan had intended to give overall command of the summer offensive to Crook, but now changed his mind.

Sheridan's scheme for the 1876 campaign called for an advance into the Powder River area by three columns under the overall tactical command of Brigadier General Alfred Howe Terry. From Fort Abraham Lincoln in the east, Terry was to lead a column centered on Custer's 7th Cavalry west to the

Right: A grizzly bear killed by Custer during the Black Hills Expedition of 1874.

Below: A view of Custer's camp at Hidden Wound Creek during the Black Hills Expedition.

Fur traders come under Indian attack on the Missouri River in about 1868.

Yellowstone River and then up the river. From Fort Shaw in the west, Colonel John Gibbon was to march a column centered on his own 7th Infantry (supported by four companies of the 2nd Cavalry), via Fort Ellis east down the Yellowstone River to meet Terry. From Fort Laramie in the south, Brigadier General George Crook was to drive a column of cavalry (parts of the 3rd and 5th Cavalry) with infantry support, via Fort Fetterman on the North Platte River, north across the Powder River toward the Bighorn River.

Sheridan's plan was to trap sizeable Indian forces in the area where the Bighorn, Rosebud, Tongue, and Powder Rivers flow northeast toward the Yellowstone River.

The Battle of Rosebud Creek

The first contact of the main campaign was also made by Crook's column. In June, the Northern Cheyenne and Sioux learned of Crook's approach down Rosebud Creek with 15 companies of cavalry and five of infantry (about 1,000 men) bolstered by 300 friendly Indians and some civilians. The Indians moved to intercept this force with some 1,500 warriors. On June 17, a squadron of the 3rd Cavalry under Captain Anson Mills was sent forward to take an Indian village, but was ambushed by the Indians and saved only by the timely arrival of a detachment from the 9th Infantry. The army vanguard then fell back on Crook's main force with the Indians pressing it hard. Soon the Indian force had swelled to between 4,000 and 6,000 warriors, and Crook's column was hard pressed to hold back the Indians in a bitterly fought six-hour battle. The Indians knew that other American columns were converging on

the area and broke off their effort against Crook to save their strength for the major battle. With his column badly mauled, Crook pulled back to his supply base at Goose Creek and refused to resume his advance until he had been reinforced.

The Battle of Rosebud Creek appeared to be an army reversal because Crook's column had withdrawn. The battle was a considerable boost to Indian morale. Moreover, major events were happening only 50 miles to the northwest, where the presence of Crook's column could have been decisive.

Terry's column had reached the Yellowstone River on June 7 and, at the point where the Powder River joins it, he established a base area supplied by river steamer. Unaware of Crook's retreat from Rosebud Creek, Terry pushed forward to link up with Gibbon slightly farther up the Yellowstone River on

June 21. Major Marcus Albert Reno was detached to lead six companies of cavalry up the Powder River. This deep reconnaissance would take them across the Tongue River and then down into the valley of Rosebud Creek.

An Elaborate, But Workable Plan

Terry convened a council of war on the steamer *Far West* and ordered a double move south, with the object of trapping the Indian main strength, which he thought was concentrated in the valley of the Little Bighorn River. To the east, Custer was to take his 7th Cavalry up the Rosebud Creek valley, cross the Wolf Mountains, and enter the Little Bighorn valley in the south. To the west, Gibbon, accompanied by Terry, was to push forward up the Bighorn River on a line

General Crook's headquarters in the field at Whitewood, Dakota Territory, during 1876.

slightly west of Custer's advance. Terry thus planned to trap the Indians between Gibbon and Custer.

Custer's specific orders were to follow the trail left by a large body of Indian ponies. If this trail veered west toward the Little Bighorn valley, he was ordered not to turn with it, but to press ahead farther south to cut the Indians' line of retreat.

Reno's force had meanwhile reached the Rosebud Creek valley. On June 17, it discovered the tracks of many ponies heading west across the Wolf Mountains in the direction of the Little Bighorn valley. Reno did not know that Crook had been checked farther up the Rosebud Creek valley earlier the same day and therefore could not inform Terry that a large part of his overall strength was not moving toward the designated rendezvous area in the Bighorn valley. Reno moved into the Little Bighorn valley and later rejoined Custer.

Custer Takes Matters Into His Own Hands

The overall plan was ruined when Custer decided not to follow Terry's orders. Custer was instructed to press on south even if the tracks his regiment was following turned west. Instead, he wheeled in the same direction and crossed the Wolf Mountains to reach the Little Bighorn valley one day ahead of Terry's schedule. As usual, Custer was supremely confident. His tactical skills as a cavalry commander had elevated him to the rank of major general at the age of 25 during the Civil War. He was also sure that the Indians would as usual scatter in the face of the cavalry's strength.

Custer did not appreciate, however, that the encampment he saw in the Little Bighorn valley was possibly the largest assembly of Indians ever seen in

The Grand Council held at General Crook's headquarters at Goose Creek on June 15, 1876.

Marcus Reno
For further references see pages 67, 71, 72, 73

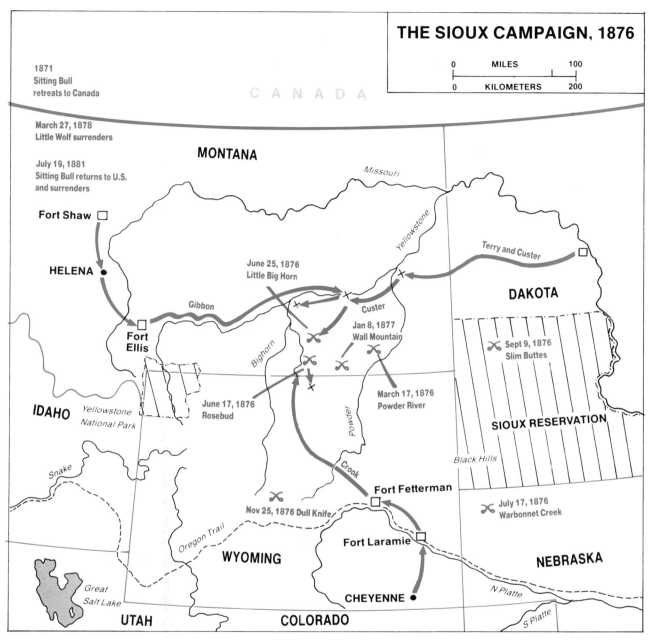

THE SIOUX CAMPAIGN, 1876

```
0        MILES        100
0      KILOMETERS      200
```

1871
Sitting Bull
retreats to Canada

CANADA

March 27, 1878
Little Wolf surrenders

July 19, 1881
Sitting Bull returns to U.S.
and surrenders

MONTANA

Missouri

Fort Shaw

HELENA

Yellowstone

Terry and Custer

DAKOTA

Gibbon

June 25, 1876
Little Big Horn

Custer

Fort
Ellis

Bighorn

Jan 8, 1877
Wall Mountain

Sept 9, 1876
Slim Buttes

IDAHO

Yellowstone
National Park

June 17, 1876
Rosebud

Powder

March 17, 1876
Powder River

SIOUX RESERVATION

Black Hills

Snake

Crook

Fort Fetterman

July 17, 1876
Warbonnet Creek

Great
Salt Lake

Nov 25, 1876 Dull Knife

Oregon Trail

Fort Laramie

NEBRASKA

WYOMING

UTAH

COLORADO

CHEYENNE

N Platte

S Platte

The Sioux campaign of 1876.

Overleaf Top: Crook's force crosses the west fork of Goose Creek on June 17, 1876, one day before the Battle of the Rosebud.

Overleaf Below: Custer's force on the move across the plains of Dakota. This view reveals cavalry, artillery, and wagons.

the plains. The camp contained perhaps 15,000 Northern Cheyennes and Sioux, including 4,000 warriors led by chiefs such as Sitting Bull, Crazy Horse, Gall, Crow King, Lame Deer, Hump, and Two Moons.

At about noon on June 25, in the face of this overwhelming Indian strength, Custer decided to follow his normal practice of dividing his command. Captain Frederick W. Benteen was sent with D, H, and K Companies to reconnoiter on Custer's left. This move was not unusual, especially against Indians who were also

elusive and likely to slip away at the first sign of a major attack. About 2½ hours later, Custer had advanced to a point about two miles from the river. There, he could see the upper end of the Indian encampment. He detached A, G, and M Companies under Reno to cross the river and charge the encampment between the river and Shoulderblade Creek, on the extreme left of the 7th Cavalry's attack. Custer himself, with C, E, F, I, and L Companies, moved off to the right in a fold of the ground that prevented him from seeing the huge size of the encamp-

Right: One of Custer's scouts was Mars-che-coodo (White Man Runs Him), a Crow Indian born in 1854. This photograph was taken in 1910 on the Crow Agency in Montana.

Below: Reputed to be the sole survivor of Custer's command at the Battle of the Little Bighorn was one of the 7th cavalry's Crow scouts, known as "Curley."

ment. Historians are uncertain about Custer's intention: the two most likely choices are a flank attack on the Indians' extreme left, or a blow at the Indians' rear once Reno's attack had pinned them down. As his five companies moved past the Indian encampment, Custer sent Sergeant Daniel Kanipe back to bring up the regimental pack train and its escorting B Company. He then detached Trumpeter John Martin to inform Benteen that a "big village" lay ahead, and to "be quick – bring packs."

The Battle of the Little Bighorn

The Battle of the Little Bighorn lasted about two hours. At 3:00 p.m., Reno started the battle. He advanced his three companies and their Arickara scouts against the southern end of the encampment, which was the location of the Hunkpapa Sioux. However, Reno's detachment met not a disorganized and fleeing enemy, but a mass of advancing Indians under the command of Gall. Full of fight after their success against Crook a week earlier, the Sioux were also

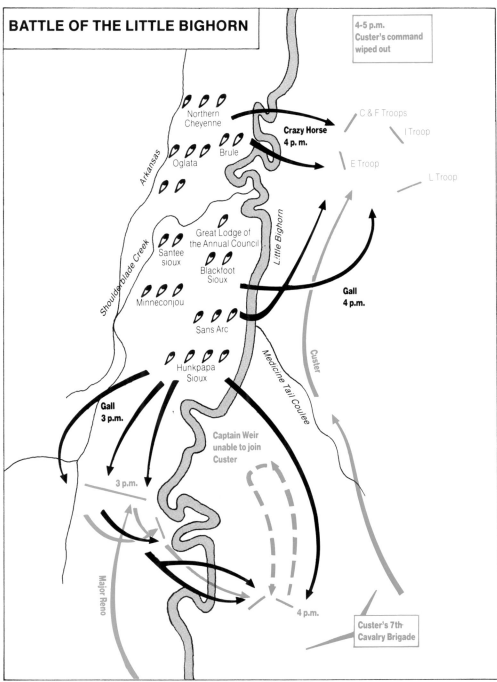

BATTLE OF THE LITTLE BIGHORN

4-5 p.m.
Custer's command wiped out

C & F Troops

I Troop

E Troop

L Troop

Crazy Horse
4 p.m.

Northern
Cheyenne

Arkansas

Oglata   Brule

Shoulderblade Creek

Great Lodge of
the Annual Council

Little Bighorn

Santee
sioux

Blackfoot
Sioux

Gall
4 p.m.

Minneconjou

Custer

Sans Arc

Medicine Tail Coulee

Hunkpapa
Sioux

Gall
3 p.m.

Captain Weir
unable to join
Custer

3 p.m.

Major Reno

4 p.m.

Custer's 7th
Cavalry Brigade

Previous Page: This stylized illustration of the Battle of the Little Bighorn cannot be too far from reality except in the terrain features Custer can be seen at the center of the American defense, with a pistol in each hand.

Left: The Battle of the Little Bighorn.

determined to check Reno's advance so that their women and children could get away. Outnumbered and in imminent danger of being overrun, Reno made the inevitable decision: he pulled his detachment back to the defensive bluffs across the river. The three companies had suffered heavy casualties by the time they reached the bluffs, but they dug in there and prepared to hold off any Indian onslaught.

About four miles to the north, Custer's 215 men reached a point opposite the end of the Indian encampment. At 4:00 p.m., they were attacked by Northern Cheyennes, Brule Sioux, and Oglala Sioux under the command of Crazy Horse. Soon, Gall arrived from the other end of the encampment. His Hunkpapa Sioux were reinforced by Blackfoot Sioux and Sans Arcs, and Custer was surrounded. By 5:00 p.m., Custer and all his men had been killed.

The Sioux had concentrated on Custer. Their preoccupation had provided Benteen's three companies and the pack train with its single company a chance to join Reno in his defensive position above the Little Bighorn River. Reno tried to move his force toward Custer, but he was uncertain of Custer's position. He turned back and reoccupied his defensive position. During the remaining daylight hours of June 25 and right through June 26, Reno's force held back determined attacks until Gibbon's column arrived and provided relief on June 27.

The Battle of the Little Bighorn was a major reverse. The 7th Cavalry had lost about half its strength (250 killed and 44 wounded). The American public was as shocked as the army and called for revenge.

Chief Sitting Bull's strength and determination are amply reflected in his implacable gaze.

The Battle of the Little Bighorn occurred on June 25, 1876. Custer split his small force into three columns and led one of them into the middle of an overwhelming number of Indians - the two detached commands did not know what happened to Custer:

When I left Gen. Custer he was at the head of a column of troops, and they were moving at a walk, and Major Reno pulled out at a trot. I had seen a portion of the Indian village before Gen. Custer and Major Reno separated.

The village was separated along the left bank of the Little Big Horn river. Owing to the bend in the stream and the timber around the left bank of the stream, as you go down the bottom, it was almost impossible, unless you got well out on the plain, to see much of the village in coming from the direction that we came. We could see some of the tepees, but it was impossible, to see the extent of it or how large the village itself was. I don't think I ever made much, or any, figures, on the strength of the Indians I had seen ... there were certainly more Indians than I ever saw together before.

It was a very large village. I could see that very plainly, because I had seen immense numbers of Indians from the tops of the bluffs I was on when I was out scouting.

We started out fifty to seventy-five yards ahead of the command. The river bottom opened out wider as we went down the stream. There was quite a large body of the Indians some little distance off, and they were running away from us, and then running back and forth across the prairie and toward us, and in every direction, apparently trying to kick up all the dust they could, and it was so covered with dust that it was impossible to discover the number of Indians there.

The Indians let us come closer and closer as we came down, and we could see about half way down to where the final halt was made, and we could see a number of Indian tepees.

We went down possibly two miles, and the line then halted and dismounted.

There certainly was a feeling of uneasiness in the command regarding Custer while we were fighting in the river bottom. I was thinking, "Has he got in the same fix we are in?" What has become of him? Has he been thrown off?" But the

idea that the command had been cut up and wiped out as it was I didn't think of such a thing. I don't know as there was any such feeling as that.

When I heard firing in the direction Custer was supposed to have gone, it was my impression that he had got to the other end of the village and struck this force of Indians that we had been fighting, and that he was having a siege of it too. The idea of Custer being killed never struck me - it never entered my mind.

Unaware of Custer's fate, the remainder of the regiment defended a hilltop. They took heavy losses but held for two days until help arrived:

The night of the 25th when the line was first formed I laid right down on the line with men while the firing was going on, and until it ceased, and as soon as it ceased I was asleep. I didn't know anything until the bullets commenced to fly around the next morning, and then I got up. The men had been fortifying in the night, or rather, digging out the little holes they did. Most of that day I lay with Capt. French in that little hole. I think we were there two or three hours anyway. In fact, the Indians were firing very rapidly at us, and we just laid still and made no reply to them whatever - just let them shoot - until they would start to make a rush on us, and then we would get up and open on them and they would go back and that thing alternated for a long time. I endeavored to get some scouts to try and get outside the lines with a dispatch, and I finally got two or three Crows to say they would go if the 'Rees would go; and I went over to see Major Reno to get a note, and I think he wrote four copies of the note, and I sent it out with the scouts. The note was not taken out. The Indian scouts did not get through the lines at all. I don't think they made any attempt to at all.

I don't know exactly how to describe the movement of the Indians on the hill. They would lie behind a ridge from 200 to 400 or 500 yards ... as the hills lay around us. There was one piece where I don't think they were 100 yards off. We had to charge on them ourselves and drive them out of there. They would lie just behind the ridge, and it would be just one line of smoke around the whole range. We would lie still and let them go on, and when they would suppose they had hurt us they would get ready and try it on again. They would come up and charge us. They would sit back on

their horses and ride up, and we would pour it into them and they would fall back. That was kept up all day long.

Opposite: ''Curley'' was one of the 7th Cavalry Regiment's Crow scouts in the Little Bighorn campaign.

Above: Photographed by a self-explanatory marker 50 years after the Battle of the Little Bighorn are White Man Runs Him and General E.S. Godfrey, who as a lieutenant had fought on the edge of the battle.

Left: The site of Major Marcus A. Reno's crossing of the Little Bighorn River on June 25, 1886, as he moved east across the river to link up with the command of Captain Frederick W. Benteen.

The Plains Indians

On the eve of the European move into North America during the first half of the 17th century, the continent was widely populated by native inhabitants of Asiatic racial origins. The native inhabitants of what are today Canada, the United States, and northern Mexico have been grouped by anthropologists into several distinct groups. The tribes of each group were characterized by a similar economic basis of life, as well as related social and political systems.

In what is now Canada and Alaska were the Arctic and Sub-Arctic groups, with the Northwest Coastal group occupying the coastal strip as far south as California. Northern Mexico was occupied by the peoples of the Southwestern group, whose Mojave, Hopi, Navajo, and Apache tribes also occupied what is now the southwest of the United States. The main part of the present United States was home to six groups, each containing several societies or tribal subgroups.

The Northeast group was located in the eastern woodlands from the Atlantic coast to points west of the Great Lakes and south of the Ohio River. These tribes included the Susquehanna, Massachusett, Narraganset, Delaware,

Typical of the tribesmen of the Great Lakes area is Kishkekosh, a Fox warrior depicted here in 1837.

Powhatan, Iroquois, Erie, Potawatomi, Fox, Miami (or Maumee), Shawnee, and Illinois.

The Southeastern group occupied the area south of the Northeastern group and as far west as Louisiana and eastern Texas. These tribes included the Catawba, Creek, Timucua, Calusa, Cherokee, Chickasaw, Choctaw, Natchez, and Caddo.

West of the Northeastern and Southeastern groups was the Great Plains group, which included the Sarci, Blackfoot, Crow, Mandan, Cheyenne, Sioux, Pawnee, Arapaho, Kiowa, Wichita, Osage, and Comanche tribes.

Northwest of this group was the Plateau group including the Shuswap and Nez Perce.

South of this group was the Great Basin group. These tribes included the Shoshoni, Paiute, and Ute.

Finally, there was the California group, whose tribes included the Yurok, Karok, Modoc, Pomo, Yokut, Chumash, and Cochimi.

These native Americans numbered about one million in 1600 and spoke about 2,000 languages. Most of the Indians lived in small villages, subsisting on maize, game, and fish. In the short term, the coming of the Europeans resulted in a flowering of Indian culture. From the arriving whites, the Indians of the Great Plains got their horses, the Navajos their sheep, and the Iroquois their weapons. But within a few years, everything went downhill for the Indians, in what has been described as the reverse of the American dream: "Expansion became contraction, democracy became tyranny, prosperity became poverty, and liberty became confinement."

The Arrival of European Settlers

The first European colony on the eastern seaboard of North America was Jamestown, which the London Company established in 1607. In the period that followed, virtually every other European country with access to the North Atlantic followed, and settlements were established by the French, Spanish, Dutch, and Swedes. These colonies grew in number, size, and importance, and soon became involved in warfare between themselves. The local tribes were inevitably affected by the wave of colonization, and several small wars were fought. This tendency was increased as the colonies became involved in conflicts that were extensions of European politics. They made alliances with tribes against colonies of other powers, which had their own Indian allies.

The tribes of New England were savagely decimated by diseases that arrived with the European colonists, and were then broken in the Pequot War (1636-37) and King Philip's War (1675-78). In the middle colonies, the powerful Delaware nation was defeated in the three phases of the Dutch-Indian Wars (1655-64) and scattered to the west in a great movement that saw the nation's dissolution as the Delawares spread in a process that now finds them in many spots between Canada and Texas. After the establishment of the United States, the southern tribes were dispossessed. Planters, led by Andrew Jackson, waged a campaign to secure legislation to remove the Indians. Despite the opposition of the Supreme Court, 50,000 Cherokee men, women, and children were herded into concentration camps and then sent on a terrible march over the "Trail of Tears" to Oklahoma in the winter of 1838-39. The same fate befell other southern tribes, notably the Choctaw, Creek, and Chickasaw peoples. Only the Seminoles held out for a time in the swamps of Florida.

The Tribes of the Great Plains

White settlers moved into the Great Plains between the Mississippi River and the Rocky Mountains. Here for the first time pioneers and soldiers encountered "cavalry" rather than "infantry" Indians in the form of the 12 major tribal societies of the Great Plains group.

These tribes, which all depended for their existence on the great herds of buffalo that roamed the plains, were also akin in using horses and tepees as the cornerstones of their nomadic existence. Other features that the Great Plains tribes had in common were the division of warriors into societies, and the religious ceremony known as the Sun Dance. There were of course considerable differences between tribes, most clearly between northern and southern tribes such as the Blackfoot and Comanche, and in areas where tribes of the Great Plains shared borders with tribes of other groups.

Tribes of the "Dog Days"

The 12 tribes established themselves on the Great Plains in a time known as the "dog days," the period before the introduction of the horse when the dog was the main beast of burden. Most of the tribes moved west from the woodlands of the east, crossing the prairies to reach the Great Plains. Though the move was made in the "dog days," after the arrival of the horse, the 12 tribes began to adopt the nomadic lifestyle during the 17th century. During this period, the tribes generally abandoned their semi-nomadic hold on the border areas and their partial reliance on farming. Instead, they lived a fully nomadic existence, the "golden age," in the center of the Great Plains, where they relied almost wholly on the buffalo.

In spite of certain characteristics common to the 12 tribes, there were many variations between them, and of course between man and man. The whole way of life stressed the significance of the individual, largely because the tribes of the Great Plains believed in the superiority of the spiritual over the material. Thus, at the core of the life of the Indian of the Great Plains was not physical survival but spiritual renewal, a condition that emphasized complete harmony with the many sacred powers. The word that has come to be used for the Indians' spiritual power is "medicine." It was the guiding element for each man's conduct in hunting, war, and all other aspects of everyday life.

Divisions and Subdivisions

In many ways, to describe the Indians of the Great Plains as being divided into 12 tribes oversimplifies the situation.

Men of the Wampanoag tribe attack a European settlement in 1675.

There were linguistic, social, and religious bonds between various tribes, but there were also divisions within each tribe into sub-tribes, clans, and hunting bands. For example, the Sioux nation, the largest of the tribes of the Great Plains, consisted of three quite distinct groups; the Dakotahs (or Santee Sioux), the Nakotas (or Yankton Sioux), and the Lakotas (or Teton Sioux). The first two remained on the eastern borders of the Great Plains, while the third moved into the center and become known as the Western Sioux.

The Western Sioux were themselves divided into seven sub-tribes, namely the Brule, Hunkpapa, Miniconjou, Oglala, Oohenonpah, Sans Arcs, and Sihasapa Sioux. Even these sub-tribes were too large to exist as concentrated groups except for a short time in the summer. In the fall, each sub-tribe split into hunting bands to pursue the buffalo, which were doing exactly the same thing as the lush grass of summer disappeared. These hunting bands were small enough to have great mobility together with minimum grazing and food needs, but large enough to defend themselves and constitute an effective buffalo-hunting force. The hunting bands generally included between 20 and 30 families. The Oglala Sioux, for example, generally split into six hunting groups known as the Oglala, Red Water, Old Skin Necklace, Night Cloud, Red Lodge, and Short Hair bands.

These bands provided survival capability from the fall, through the winter, to the beginning of the summer, when the tribe reassembled for large hunts and religious ceremonies including the Sun Dance which reaffirmed the tribe's dedication to the spirits of earth, air, and nature.

Marriage usually took place outside the hunting group. This reduced the chance of inbreeding, with its potentially harmful long-term implications. It also helped to bond the various groups, so the annual summer assembly became a major family reunion as well as a tribal event. Polygamy was normal among the tribes of the Great Plains, for in a warrior society of this type, women outnumbered men by far. Women were also the generators of wealth in the form of trade goods such as buffalo hide, robes and dressed furs.

The Bison Dance of the Mandan tribe.

The Place of the Chiefs

In the complete tribe and its sub-tribes, and the hunting bands, considerable emphasis was placed on harmonious relations within the group. Such relations were the task of the various chiefs, who were in effect heads of families. The two types of leader were the civil chief and the war chief, supported by groups of elders and the shamans ("medicine men"). Civil chiefs were in general older men, and their responsibility was the day-to-day life of the group, regardless of whether it was a hunting group or a tribe. The war chiefs were the officers of the various warrior societies, concerned only with military matters.

Chiefs, whether civil or war, did not have any overriding authority but depended on personal strength of character. Authority was therefore gained by men with strength of character and the perceived virtues of a good man. These virtues were generally considered to be good sense, personal honesty, an even temperament, a sense of responsibility, and considerable generosity. Even with a full set of these virtues, the chief was still regarded more as the chairman of the board than as the chief executive. Matters affecting the tribe were the responsibility of the tribal council such as the Cheyennes' Council of Forty-Four. This body, made up of 40 chiefs from the tribe's ten hunting bands together with four Old Man Chiefs, operated within a set of well-established rules. Though its members had become chiefs through their personal qualities and influence, the council met each summer to make tribal decisions that were inevitably democratic. The council members knew that their decisions would only be implemented if they reflected the desires of the tribe as a whole.

Below Left: Medicine Crow of the Crow tribe.

Below: Chief Sitting Bull of the Sioux was one of the major forces behind Indian opposition to white encroachment on the northern part of the Great Plains.

The Importance of Personal Standing

Beloew Right: Chief Joseph was a leader of the Nez Perce, a tribe of the Plateau group which moved across the northern part of the Great Plains in its epic trek to reach Canada. Chief Joseph was probably the finest tactician produced by the Indians.

Below: Chief Kicking Bear of the Miniconjou Sioux was photographed during 1896 in his shirt decorated with human scalps.

The core of the virtues perceived by the tribesmen of the Great Plains was personal integrity, according to the tribe's intertwined social and moral values. Moreover, just as a man could rise in prestige, influence, and importance by displaying such virtues, another could be effectively excluded from the tribe if he was considered lazy, cowardly, selfish, or dishonest. These characteristics were seen by many tribes as vices. The Blackfeet sometimes subjected such men to public mockery and abuse so harsh that they went into voluntary exile or took to the warpath; the Crows made such men "joking relatives" who were expected to help each other break out of the character mold that did not accord with tribal standards. If these lesser measures did not prove effective, the council could, in the extreme, exile a man, or order his tepee and possessions to be destroyed.

The Tepee or Lodge

The tepee, or lodge, was at the center of life for the tribes of the Great Plains. The circular base of this structure, had religious connotations according with the Indians' concept of a circular world and circular family. This relationship to the spiritual world was enhanced by the practice of painting visionary experiences as well as war exploits on the cover, door, and liner. Thus, moving to any new tepee required considerable ritual.

The tepee was basically a cone tilted away from the prevailing wind. It consisted of four main poles lashed together just below their overlapping tops with sinew, a number of lighter, strengthening

poles between the main poles, and a covering of dressed buffalo hide. The lower section had an inner layer of buffalo hide to serve as a insulating draft stopper, and the narrow entrance on the eastern side was covered with a buffalo-hide flap.

The tepee provided excellent protection against the weather, could withstand virtually all conditions of wind, rain, and snow, and was easily mended. It was also extremely mobile, and the use of the horse as a draft animal meant that longer poles could be moved, making possible a tepee with an average base diameter of 15 feet.

Only two or three horses were needed to carry the covering and drag the poles of such a tepee. Erecting and dismantling was the task of women, and two skilled women could raise or pack a tepee in a very short time. At the tepee's top were two smoke flaps, positioned by exterior poles, according to the strength and direction of the wind. They provided air circulation to allow ventilation and made a chimney to give an exit for smoke from the central fire. The lower part of the cover could be rolled up to provide additional movement of air in the hot summer months.

Tepees on the Umatilla Reservation, photographed at the end of the 19th century.

Different Roles for Men and Women

Within the nomadic villages of the Great Plains tribes, the responsibilities of men and women were sharply divided. The women were responsible for raising the children, maintaining and transporting the tepee, organizing the tepee and keeping it neat inside, preparing and serving meals, and dressing and subsequently working skins. This last was a particularly hard job, for the skins were heavy and difficult to handle. The whole process involved cleaning, curing, scraping, and tanning the skins before the women could then set to work turning the skins into all manner of useful items. Women also devoted considerable time, ingenuity, and artistic skill to decorative work such as quilling and, after 1830 when trade beads became widespread, beading. There were women's guilds specializing in these crafts, and these skills were so highly regarded that particularly gifted women had prestige equal to that of great warriors.

The responsibilities of the women were particularly heavy. Those of the men – not as arduous, but considerably more dangerous – were hunting and fighting. Though other creatures were hunted (antelope and deer for their meat and skins, beaver and weasel for their furs, and birds for their feathers), it was the buffalo that lay at the very core of the Indians' existence on the Great Plains. In the days before the horse, hunting buffalo had been a cooperative effort, on foot, to drive the animals into a stockade (with a sharp drop or an icy slope as entrance) or over a cliff. The horse transformed the Indians' ability to hunt the buffalo effectively.

Buffalo hunting

The two primary methods were the surround and the chase. The surround was a development of the tactic used in pre-horse days to drive part of the buffalo herd into the stockade or over the drop. The hunters approached the buffalo herd from downwind in two lines or an arc, and then joined

Before the advent of the horse, the Indians compensated for their lack of mobility in the hunt by clever tricks such as the use of animal skins as shown in this German illustration.

Plains life had a savage beauty. This painting by Charles Russell captures the rhythm between horse and man.

up into a yelling circle that was gradually tightened around the animals. The beasts panicked easily, and, as they milled around inside the cordon of hunters, they were easily picked off with arrow and lance. Casualties among the hunters were almost inevitable, but were regarded as the price that had to be paid.

The chase made more effective use of the mobility provided by the horse. The hunters approached the buffalo from downwind as quietly as possible and on a signal, charged straight at the herd. Panicking, the animals turned and ran, spreading apart as they tried to outrun the hunters. The hunters used specially trained "buffalo runners," horses which responded to pressure from the rider's knees and did not flinch in the presence of a massive buffalo. As the hunter approached his quarry, the horse came up on the buffalo's right side if the

rider was a right-handed archer or, in the rarer case that the hunter was using a lance, on the animal's left side. When he was in position, the rider shot or stabbed the buffalo behind the last rib to pierce its vital organs. The horse was trained to veer away as soon as it heard the twang of the bowstring, but then gallop parallel to the quarry in case more arrows were needed. The average hunter could bring down two buffaloes before his horse was outdistanced, but exceptional hunters were often credited with four or five buffaloes. Most hunters preferred to use the bow, and the individual arrow markings used by each man guaranteed that the kills were credited to the right hunter. The hunt was communal, but the identification of kills allowed hunters to build up their personal prestige.

Tribal hunts were standard during the summer, but the declining size of the herds

during the fall meant that the tribes broke up into hunting bands between August and November. Each band then moved into an area with enough game for its needs, shifting only when it had exhausted local supplies. The bands finally settled into individual winter encampments, where they survived on dried meat supplemented by any game that could be found locally. Only if the grazing for the horses ran out, or if starvation was imminent, did the band move its winter camp. Movement resumed in the spring, and early in summer the bands began to drift toward the designated annual assembly point for the whole tribe.

Annual Assembly

The bands camped in a fixed order around the council tepee. The purest form of such a camp was that of the Cheyennes, with the First (or Aorta) Band southeast of the council tepee. The Second (or Hairy) Band, the Third (or Scabby) Band, the Fourth (or Half Cheyenne) Band, and the Fifth (or Dog Men) Band ran clockwise from this point. The summer assembly was an occasion for reunions, consolidation of tribal unity, councils, and religious ceremonies.

The horse which transformed the life of the Indians on the Great Plains arrived from the south. The Spaniards had introduced the horse to the areas now known as northern Mexico, New Mexico, and Texas. They trained the local Pueblo Indians in the art of horse handling, and from the Pueblos this knowledge passed to neighboring tribes such as the Apaches. Trade, straying, and theft gradually extended the range of the horse northward into the southern part of the Great Plains, and

The nature of the country and its bounty dictated a different lifestyle for the Indian tribes of the northwest, as shown in this illustration of net fishing on the Columbia River.

83

many thousands of animals were freed by the Pueblo Revolt of 1680. By 1700, the horse's range had stretched north to the Kiowas and Comanches, and west to the Shoshones and Utes; by 1750, the Sioux, Cheyennes, Crows, and Blackfoot all had the horse. By 1770, all the tribes of the Great Plains kept horses.

The Horse Reaches the Great Plains

On first contact with the horse, the tribes were generally awed. But soon they came to see that the horse was an animal able to undertake the draft role of the dog, but with considerably superior speed and endurance, as well as a much greater load, one that could include a man. The horse extended each tribe's potential hunting grounds. It also made a period of constant tribal warfare possible. This con-

flict seldom took the form of large battles, but harassing raids often made the life of the target tribe so unbearable that it would decamp and leave its hunting grounds to the victor.

The raids were not meant to involve bloodshed, for the men of the small raiding parties thought it better to steal the enemy's horses if possible. Success in such raids improved the importance of the tribe and increased the prestige of the men involved, especially if they succeeded in capturing particularly prized animals such as war or buffalo horses.

The horse made warfare more practical, and therefore more probable, for the tribes of the Great Plains. It also allowed the rapid evolution of a truly nomadic life through more effective hunting and the ability to move larger loads. In short, it was the horse that created the tribes of the Great Plains that the settlers encountered as they

A Blackfoot using his horse to pull a travois. The horse was obviously far better suited for such tasks than the dogs which were used before the advent of the horse in Indian life.

moved west from the Mississippi and Missouri rivers.

The Bellicose Warrior

The tribes were certainly warlike. This bellicosity had its origins in a number of factors, including the need to win and keep the best tribal ranges, complete with good campsites and hunting grounds. Just as important, however, was the desire of the tribes to make themselves secure through a combination of aggression and self-assertion. This did not mean the use of large war parties to crush weak opponents. Instead, small war parties were sent deep into the lands of the tribe's most powerful opponents for daring raids. This tactic would be regarded today as reckless, and may not have served any useful military purpose;

but by the standards prevailing on the Great Plains, it served two purposes: it lowered the morale of their opponents, and it raised their own morale through the physical and moral assertion of their own bravery, strength and, most important, "medicine."

It is clear, therefore, that for the Indians of the Great Plains a major part of war was the display of fearlessness, which was proved by the way individual warriors fought. In combat, killing an opponent played a secondary part to the display of personal skill and daring. The greatest prestige went to those warriors who showed the highest contempt for their opponents, a situation that completely mirrored the tribal belief in self-assertion.

It was in conflict that the warrior really proved his worth and gained prestige. The running of risks brought fame, and it was

This 1891 photograph of the Sioux camp at the Brule River, near the Pine Ridge Reservation of South Dakota, reveals that despite the intrusion of some outside influences (such as the wagons), much of the tribe's domestic life remained unaltered.

universally believed that to be killed in battle was far better than to die in bed of old age or disease. Under a set of complicated motives that are difficult to define, but which were fully – if intuitively – understood by their exponents, the warfare of the Great Plains had a number of forms. Defensive warfare was concerned with protecting the tribe or hunting group. Because it was forced on the tribe or hunting group from outside, it was very different from offensive warfare, which was itself divided into two basic types, the scalp raid and the horse raid.

Two Types of Offensive Warfare

The scalp raid was designed to kill the enemy's warriors. Before the advent of the horse, such battles were generally exchanges of arrows at long range or, less frequently, attacks on small camps by a large force. The arrival of the horse reduced the tendency toward scalp raids,

and major clashes became rarer still.

The main motives for a scalp raid were revenge and the desire to complete a period of mourning in a fitting manner. This type of raid was highly organized, and as such involved considerable ritual. Many promises and sacrifices were made to the sacred powers in an effort to guarantee success, and the warriors wore their full fighting regalia and paraded with their favorite horses in variants of the Big Dance or Horseback Dance to help boost the tribe's fighting spirit. The raiders were generally relatives of the man being mourned, and their successful return was usually celebrated with a Scalp Dance, which varied considerably from tribe to tribe, but had the common feature of celebrating the returned warriors' skill and bravery. Enemy scalps were displayed on poles, which were often carried by women, the raiders' coups were recounted, and frequently a scalp was offered to the relatives of the avenged man.

A sioux charge in the Battle of Rosebud Creek (1876), directed against a cavalry detatchment commanded by William B. Royall.

The horse raid was more common, but less organized. The number of warriors involved was smaller, and the raids were often undertaken without the knowledge or permission of the tribe's chiefs. This kind of raid provided the best opportunity for a warrior to prove his courage, and to build up his prestige and wealth by seizing horses from the enemy. There was some ceremony before the raiders departed, but it was undertaken on a personal level.

The capture of horses was one way in which a warrior could improve his prestige. Another was the "coup." In its highest form, the coup involved just touching an opponent with the hand or something held in the hand, such as a weapon, a quirt, or a "coup stick," a special willow wand designed specifically for the purpose. A classic example of coup was achieved at the Battle of the Little Bighorn by Yellow Nose, a Cheyenne warrior, who seized Custer's standard and use it to "count coup" on American soldiers. There were other acts which were classed as coups and which permitted the warrior to decorate his body, clothes, and horse with symbols indicating his prestige. Different tribes had different standards and different systems of grading. The Crows, for example, thought most highly of the warrior who

Above: Chief Big Foot played a major, and ultimately disastrous, part in the final Sioux uprising of 1890.

Right: In this early illustration, tribesmen of the Northeastern group in the eastern woodlands counter with European allies in an effort to decide the fate of a captive European family.

coups by the Crees and Sioux, but lower by the other tribes of the Great Plains. There was also a spiritual dimension; the hair was part of the identity of an enemy, and as such was an extension of the soul.

Weapons of the Great Plains

Until their contact with the white man, who introduced them to the gun and metal-bladed weapons, the Indians had been restricted to the bow, lance, and club as their weapons. The most important was the bow, which in its definitive form for use by a mounted warrior or hunter, was between three and four feet long. Bows were sometimes made of horn, but more frequently of wood with a strengthening of sinew, which was also used for the string. A good bow, especially the reflex type which had considerably more power than a simple bow, was a prized possession. So too were straight arrows, whose original flint or stone heads were later replaced by metal heads obtained from white traders. The bows of the Great Plains were very powerful, especially those made of composite wood, horn, and sinew. They could fire arrows with enough force to pass through a buffalo or a man's head.

The Great Plains warrior and hunter was as skilled with his bow as he was with his horse. He rode from an early age and acquired a natural mastery of riding, he also practiced with the bow from childhood. Most warriors developed great accuracy at a range of about 100 yards when they shot from a galloping horse. In general, however, they tried to narrow the range whenever possible.

The Indians took to the musket and then the rifle when they became available. Early trade weapons were generally heavy and inaccurate, so the Indians often preferred the bow for its accuracy as well as its quietness and higher rate of fire. Owning a firearm conferred considerable prestige, but only after faster firing and more accurate mass-produced breech-loading weapons became avail-

had led a raid, captured a picketed horse, counted coup, and seized a gun from an enemy's hand. The Blackfeet thought snatching a gun was worthy of the highest prestige and ranked this act above the killing of an enemy.

Circumstance also played a major part in deciding the value of a coup. Greatest significance was placed on a coup against a warrior of note, or a coup carried out within the enemy's camp. The first coup of any battle counted for more than later coups, and several coups could be counted on the same individual opponent, although each successive coup counted less than the one before: the Arapahos and Sioux allowed four coups against a single warrior, while the Cheyennes permitted only three.

Like the stolen horse and snatched gun, the scalp was considered tangible proof of prowess in war. The scalping of an enemy was thought higher than other

The impact of the settlers on the way of life of the tribes of the Great Plains is provided by this 1870 photograph of Chief Asa-to-yet of the Comanches, who was known to the Americans as Will Soule.

Morning Star, known to the army as Dull Knife, was a chief of the Northern Cheyennes. The village of his band on the canyon bed of Crazy Woman's Fork of the Powder River was destroyed on November 25, 1876, as part of the U.S. offensive after the Battle of the Little Bighorn.

able in the late 1860s did the bow fade into a secondary role.

The main defensive item was the shield, which was circular. From a diameter of about 36 inches in the "dog days" the shield was reduced to between 18 and 24 inches after the arrival of the horse. The shield was made of one or two layers of buffalo hide shrunk by heating and often had padding of hair or feather. The shield could stop an arrow or low-velocity bullet, but its real strength was thought to lie in the "medicine" of the patterns painted on it. Indeed, this "medicine," was so significant that warriors often carried only the thin outer part or even a scaled-down model with an accurate rendition of the full-size shield's markings.

Warrior Societies

In the tribes of the Great Plains, the warriors were organized into societies that were both social organizations and

A decisive figure in the eventual destruction of the Indian way of life on the Great Plains was George Armstrong Custer, seen here as a major general at the end of the Civil War.

Opposite: Short Bull, a Sioux, wearing an armor tunic made of wood.

military units through which a warrior could advance through various ranks that brought increasing prestige. Each society met regularly, and had its own dances, songs, and dress.

The two types of warrior society were the graded society and non-graded society. The graded society was the type adopted by the Arapaho, Blackfoot, Gros Ventre, Hidatsa, Kiowa, and Mandan tribes. As a group of boys reached the age at which they could fight, they offered a pipe and other gifts to the youths next up in age from them, who were the members of the most junior society, and so bought the right to that society's dances, songs, rituals, and regalia. As new members of the society, the boys were taught the rituals. Then, the original members left the society to its new members and bought their way into the

society next up in seniority. So each warrior progressed gradually over the years into the most senior society, and finally retired as a warrior after selling his membership.

The non-graded society was adopted by the Arikara, Assiniboin, Crow, Cheyenne, Pawnee, and Sioux tribes. In this system, the societies were theoretically of equal status, though evidence of rivalry is provided by the fact that societies sought to entice celebrated warriors into their ranks with gifts.

Such then were the people of the tribes on the Great Plains. They had existed in this form for perhaps only 100 years since the horse had been integrated into their way of life, but the beautiful balance of this way of life inevitably collapsed under the pressure of white immigration.

Left: Rain in the Face, the man thought to have killed Custer.

Below: The only living thing left on the site of the 7th Cavalry's defeat at the Little Big Horn was Comanche, Custer's horse.

The Fight at War Bonnet Creek

Colonel W. Merritt was already moving into the area with his 5th Cavalry to support Crook. On July 17, Merritt met a band of Northern Cheyennes at War Bonnet. Chief Yellow Knife was killed by "Buffalo Bill" Cody, and Merritt forced the Indians to move to the Red Cloud Agency. On August 3, Merritt linked up with Crook, and the two colonels moved north with their forces to meet Terry on August 10 in the Rosebud Creek valley. Terry however decided to abandon the campaign and returned east.

Crook was given permission to remain in the field on what soon became known as the "Starvation March." Crook continued harassing the Indians until his rations were exhausted. He then sent Captain Mills with a company of the 3rd Cavalry to Deadwood for further supplies. Mills departed on September 7, but was

COL.W.F.CODY

I AM COMING

"Colonel" W.F.Cody was a key player in the closing stages of the Sioux wars.

then pinned down at Slim Buttes two days later until Crook arrived with the rest of his force. After picking up supplies, Crook continued his policy of harassments with several columns even after the onset of winter.

On November 14, Crook departed from Fort Fetterman along the abandoned Bozeman Trail, and on November 25, he successfully fought the Battle of Crazy Woman Fork. Crook discovered a large Indian encampment and gave the task of destroying it to ten companies of cavalry under Mackenzie. They executed a brilliant night attack in temperatures well below freezing. Another commander, Colonel Miles, was also involved in the campaign of harassment. On January 8, 1877, Miles and his force of 500 infantrymen and two light guns in covered wagons located Crazy Horse's winter camp on a virtually inaccessible bluff on Wolf's Mountain. The shells of Miles's guns stampeded both the Indians and

their horses, however, and Crazy Horse soon surrendered. The Sioux war chief later escaped, but was recaptured on September 7 and died in captivity.

The Exhausted Sioux Surrender

The war was now all but over. Many Sioux were physically and mentally exhausted by the harassment of Crook and Miles. The constant threat to the women and children, combined with the fact that the warriors were sick, hungry, cold, and virtually out of ammunition, produced a steady spate of surrenders. By the spring of 1877, there was only one force of Sioux left in the field, and it was now divided. One part headed for Rosebud Creek; the other moved into Canada under Sitting Bull. In the so-called Battle of Muddy Creek on May 7, the Rosebud Creek party was dispersed by a company of the 2nd Cavalry with some infantry support, and

A company of Indian scouts in the 1876 campaign against the Chiricahua Apaches. Such scouts were generally both effective and loyal.

Modoc Indians
For further references
see pages
96, 97, 98, 99, 100

the survivors were hunted down in the summer of 1877. The war was officially declared at an end on July 16, 1877.

Sitting Bull's party remained peacefully in Canada until 1881, when a famine forced it to return to the United States. Sitting Bull surrendered at Fort Buford, North Dakota, on July 19, 1881, and moved onto a reservation.

The Great Plains was the huge area in which the largest part of the Indian Wars took place, but they were by no means the only region where the arrival of Eastern settlers sparked trouble with the peoples already inhabiting the region.

The northwestern United States, in the region now occupied by northern California, Oregon, Washington, and Idaho, had already seen limited but widespread warfare after the first large-scale intrusion by settlers in the early 1850s. During the Civil War, there was reduced intrusion by settlers and therefore of Indian reaction,

with only the 1863 campaign against the Shoshones in Idaho recorded. Immigration resumed after the war, along with further trouble, between 1865 and 1868 in northern California, southern Oregon, Idaho, and Nevada.

The Modoc War

From the late 1860s, to the early 1870s, there was an uneasy peace until the outbreak in 1872 of the Modoc War, one of the smallest, and certainly one of the oddest, campaigns the U.S. Army ever had to fight. As usual, problems arose from political pressure exerted by land-hungry settlers; in this instance, they wanted the fertile lands of the Modoc tribe of northern California. As a result, the Modocs were ordered from their ancestral lands to a reservation in southern Oregon, which they were to

Above: Though fairly small in scale compared with other deserts in the Southwest, the area of lava beds around Lake Tule provide some of the most rugged terrain conceivable for irregular warfare by comparatively small forces. The Modocs took superb advantage of this fact.

Left: Hot, dry, and immensley difficult on feet, bodies and clothing, the lava beds were a nightmare for army troops involved in the Modoc War.

Right: American light howitzers in a position with makeshift protection during the Modoc War. Artillery generally proved ineffective in this campaign, since it was virtually impossible to reach the enemy in the deep ravines and gullies they used for protection.

Below: The small but bitter Modoc War attracted considerable newspaper and magazine attention, and the reporters suffered just the same privations as the soldiers whose effort they were covering.

share with the more numerous Klamath tribe. The Modoc and Klamath had a long standing antipathy to each other and placing the two tribes on a single reservation inevitably produced friction.

In 1872, a small number of Modocs left the reservation under the leadership of a man known as Captain Jack and returned to their traditional homeland in the Lost River country of northern California. In November, 1872, the army attempted to take the Modocs back to the reservation. The local military unit was a detachment of the 1st Cavalry at Fort Klamath under Major John Green, who sent a party under Captain James Jackson to round up the Modocs. The Modocs resisted and, during the fighting, Captain Jack escaped with a small number of warriors and their families. They headed for a natural fortress, the lava beds south of Tule Lake that offered the possibility of a sustained defense. Here, Captain Jack's band was joined by dissidents from another Modoc settlement. They raised his strength to between 50 and 70 warriors, as well as some 150 women and children.

Above: An army Indian scout keeps watch during the Modoc War.

Right: One of the army's Indian scouts in the Modoc War. "Scarface Charley" was one of the Modoc leaders.

Known to the Indians as the "Land of the Burnt Out Fires," the lava beds are an extraordinary geological feature about eight miles long and four miles wide. They offered Captain Jack and his followers exceptional possibilities for a defensive stand.

The first efforts to extract the Modocs were made by civilian posses. They were unsuccessful, but they provided time for the army to concentrate a force of 400 men from the 1st Cavalry, 21st Infantry, and three militia companies (two from Oregon and one from California) under Wheaton. There were many skirmishes between the Modocs and the army; the following outline of the most important actions reveals the skill of the Indians in this type of fighting.

The Battle of the Lava Beds

At dawn on January 17, 1873, the army began trying to dislodge the Modocs. The confident soldiers exclaimed that they would have "Modoc steak" for breakfast.

97

Brigadier General Frank Wheaton (center, with a white plume on his cap) with some of his officers and their families at Fort Walla Walla in 1874.

The soldiers fought all day in the so-called Battle of the Lava Beds, but their fight was against the terrain, not against the Modocs, whom they saw hardly ever. Yet, throughout the day, the Modocs fired on the soldiers from concealed positions. When the exhausted Americans pulled back at nightfall, they had suffered nine dead and 30 wounded, most of them in Major Mason's battalion of regular infantry.

Wheaton reported that at least 1,000 men would be needed. While extra men were sent forward under Colonel Alvan Cullem Gillem of the 1st Cavalry, Wheaton was replaced by Brigadier General Edward Richard Sprigg Canby, commanding the Department of Columbia. Canby decided to try negotiation, but on April 11, 1873, the army's peace commissioners, including Canby, were treacherously killed during the talks. At the same time, a sneak attack was launched against the headquarters of the army detachment, but failed. The

Modocs' intention had been to kill all senior army and civilian personnel in the belief that the soldiers would then withdraw and leave the Modocs alone.

The high command now recognized that Wheaton's earlier demand for 1,000 men and light artillery was justified, and a small, but methodical, campaign to reduce the Modoc stronghold began. On April 15, Gillem launched a major effort. It reflected the Battle of the Lava Beds in everything, except that the soldiers were now prepared for the terrain and the tactics of the Modocs. Slowly, the soldiers fought their way forward with the increasingly effective support of some newly arrived mortars. The weapons soon found the range and shells began landing in the main Modoc stronghold. One of the shells did not explode on impact, but as one of the Indians tried to draw the fuse with his teeth, the device finally detonated, killing several of the inquisitive Indians.

Over a period of three days, the army closed in on Captain Jack's stronghold, which had been cut off from the water of Tule Lake since the beginning of the attack. Finally, on April 17, the soldiers stormed over the last ridges into the Modoc camp, only to find it deserted. The Modocs had made a getaway through an underground passage. The battle had cost eight soldiers killed and 17 wounded; eleven Modoc dead (three men and eight women) were found.

The surviving members of Captain Jack's band had escaped east to another area of ravines in the lava beds. About 85 men, including 15 Warm Spring Indian scouts, were detached on April 21 under Captain Evan Thomas to find the escapees, but were ordered not to engage them. Most of the men were from the 12th Infantry and 4th Artillery; by now, they had a healthy respect for the tactical skills of the Modoc. Even so, the detachment was ambushed by the Modocs during a meal halt. With fire from hidden marksmen pouring into their position, some of the men let their respect for the Modocs' skills turn to fear.

They fled back to the main camp. The result was a major reverse for the army, for the 85-man detachment lost 22 killed and 18 wounded. All six of the officers were hit. Five died, and only Acting Assistant Surgeon B.G. Semig survived despite two grievous wounds. It was later discovered that the ambush party numbered only 21 men, of whom not one was wounded.

A Scientifically Planned Siege

Colonel Jefferson Columbus Davis took command of the task of crushing the Modoc resistance, and he decided to reinstate Wheaton. After reorganizing his forces and bringing up supplies, Davis launched a scientifically planned campaign to trap the Modocs. He planned to occupy the ridges of the lava beds, so tightening the noose around Captain Jack's band. The Modoc, meanwhile, had divided into two parties with different objectives; one under Captain Jack and

The treacherously arranged murder of Brigadier General Canby during the Modoc War.

Hooker Jim wanted to fight; the other to escape.

Under Davis's siege, Captain Jack's party was soon in dire straits. It was practically surrounded, had been forced to move away from its water supply, and was fast running out of food and ammunition. Captain Jack decided that he and his men had to escape to the east. They intended to pass around Tule Lake to reach Oregon. On May 10, a break-out was launched by Captain Jack and 33 Modocs, but they ran into a detachment of the 4th Cavalry and 4th Artillery near Sorass Lake. The Indians managed to stampede the soldiers' horses, but Captain H.C. Hasbrouck rallied his men and drove off the Modoc. The soldiers suffered two killed and seven wounded to one Modoc killed, but the action was the army's first success against the Modocs, who had been driven off and lost 24 pack animals carrying most of their ammunition.

The divisions within the Modocs now came to a head, and the survivors divided into two groups to make their separate ways north. The Indians were now in the open, and the advantage swayed to the army. A vigorous pursuit was immediately organized, and on May 22 the less warlike party of about 100 persons was captured. Davis persuaded some of the captured Modocs to tell him Captain Jack's intentions, and he maintained a close pursuit and gradually captured small groups of the fleeing warriors.

Captain Jack Pays the Ultimate Penalty

Captain Jack was finally seized at Willow Creek Canyon on June 1. Davis planned to hang him immediately, but orders from Washington halted his summary execution. Six warriors were tried and sentenced to death, though two had their sentences reduced to life imprisonment. Captain Jack and the other three were hanged on October 3 at Fort Klamath; the others were transferred to a reservation at Baxter Springs, Kansas.

The Modoc War had been small, but

Strong liquor was a growing problem for the Indians. This illustration shows a group of Plains Indians trying to lap up a consignment of contraband whiskey intercepted and destroyed by the authorities.

The Modoc War.

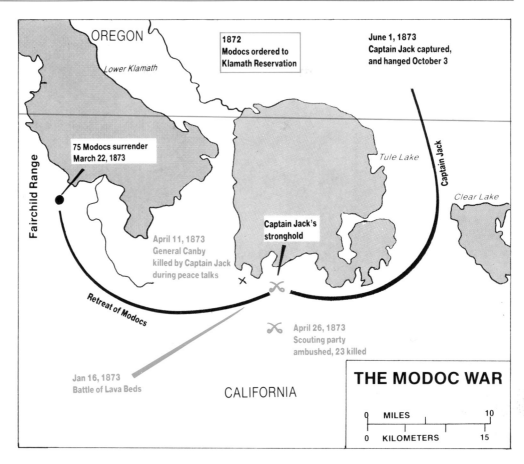

OREGON

Lower Klamath

1872
Modocs ordered to
Klamath Reservation

June 1, 1873
Captain Jack captured,
and hanged October 3

75 Modocs surrender
March 22, 1873

Fairchild Range

Tule Lake

Captain Jack

Clear Lake

Captain Jack's
stronghold

April 11, 1873
General Canby
killed by Captain Jack
during peace talks

Retreat of Modocs

April 26, 1873
Scouting party
ambushed, 23 killed

Jan 16, 1873
Battle of Lava Beds

CALIFORNIA

THE MODOC WAR

| 0 | MILES | 10 |
| 0 | KILOMETERS | 15 |

costly. It should have emphasized again the scale of the problems created when tribes were uprooted from their ancestral lands. Yet, it failed to halt settlement, with the inevitable result: another conflict in the northwest in 1877.

The Nez Perce War

Since 1863, the government had been trying to move the Nez Perce tribe from their traditional homeland along the Salmon and Wallowa Rivers, in Idaho and Oregon respectively, to the Lapwai Reservation on the Snake River in north western Idaho. The Nez Perce had refused to be transplanted with a steady courage, but in 1876, in response to incidents in which three settlers had died, the army moved into the western part of the Nez Perce homeland. The plan was to shift the most resistant group of Nez Perce under Chief Thunder-Rolling-Over-the-Mountain (known as Chief Joseph) out of Wallowa region. After some fighting,

Joseph led his people east to link up with the Nez Perce on the Salmon River.

The Battle of White Bird Canyon

Determined to punish the tribe for its actions, the army sent four officers and 90 troops of the 1st Cavalry from Fort Lapwai, who were soon joined by 11 civilians. On June 17, their force blundered into White Bird Canyon, where Joseph had laid an ambush with 200 warriors. The Battle of White Bird Canyon was a small but bloody reverse for the army, which suffered 40 percent casualties before the survivors extricated themselves. Joseph had never before been involved in warfare, for the Nez Perce were a generally peaceful tribe, but the battle should have alerted the army that Joseph would be an enemy of tactical genius.

After the battle, Joseph departed east with his entire tribe of 700 people (including only 300 warriors) on an epic search for a new homeland in Idaho or Montana.

Nez Perce Indians
For further references
see pages
101, 103, *104*, 105, 106,
107, 108

Trooper, 10th Cavalry Regiment, U.S. Army, 1880.

Heat was always a major problem in the Great Plains during the summer. In an effort to ease the plight of soldiers in the area, flannel shirts were issued from 1874. The first style tried was made of gray material with a laydown collar and no pocket, but the definitive 1877 pattern had a pocket and a ring collar. This trooper also wears the Model 1875 hat and a cartridge belt designed for use with metal cartridges. In front of the trooper (on the left-hand side of the 1872 version of the old 1859 McClellan saddle) are his blanket roll, tent half, and overcoat with spare clothing rolled inside, and a brush and shoe pouch. A forage sack with oats or corn, a saddlebag with personal kit and spare ammunition, and a canteen can be seen behind the trooper.

OH! OH! HOWARD!
"I am still pursuing the Indians."—*Telegram from General O. O. Howard.*

This cartoon reveals more than a little of the exasperation felt by the average American about the apparently slow progress of General Howard's pursuit of the Nez Perce.

Helena with one howitzer and about 200 men (six companies of his own 7th Infantry and volunteers) in wagons.

The Battle of Big Hole Basin

Joseph had thought he was safe and posted no sentries, so Gibbon's three-pronged attack at dawn on August 9, came as a complete surprise. In 20 minutes, the army had seized the encampment, but Joseph rallied his men beside the river. Exploiting the superior range and accuracy of his warriors' rifles he picked off American officers. The Nez Perce then launched several charges and finally drove back Gibbon's men, who entrenched themselves on a small hill behind the encampment. All day the Battle of Big Hole raged, with neither side able to win a complete advantage. Gibbon had sent a galloper to speed Howard's column to the area and had to survive until relief arrived.

The Nez Perce continued to snipe at the dug-in soldiers, and had disabled their only piece of artillery. Joseph then set fire to the dry prairie grass upwind of the soldiers' position, and only a last-minute change in the wind's direction saved Gibbon's survivors from being burned alive. On the third day, Howard arrived with two companies of cavalry; but Joseph, warned by his scouts, had vanished with his tribe during the night.

The Battle of Big Hole cost Gibbon 29 killed and 40 wounded, while the Nez Perce had 89 dead, including some women and children lost in the initial assault. The Nez Perce had only just failed to score a major victory and were now well ahead of their pursuers as they continued southeast from Montana into Idaho.

The army commanders realized that they needed a larger force to trap and defeat the Nez Perce, but none was readily available; the frontier had been stripped of regulars to bolster militia units involved in labor disputes that were

Throughout the Nez Perce War, the warriors under Chief Joseph consistently out-thought the pursuing troops at every level of tactical warfare. They frequently surprised their enemies in a fashion that makes Chief Joseph probably the finest tribal tactician of all.

paralyzing the east. The wounded Gibbon and most of his men were out of the running, which left just the dogged Howard.

Howard reckoned that the Nez Perce were headed for Yellowstone National Park. He detached Lieutenant George R. Bacon with a small number of men to block the Indians' line of advance in Tacher's Pass. Joseph now had another chance to display his steadily improving tactical genius. Grouping 45 of his mounted warriors into fours, he approached Howard's camp on Camas Creek during the night of August 18. As

Joseph had expected, the sentries mistook the Nez Perce for Bacon's party returning after a fruitless journey. The alarm was raised only as the Indians swept into the army camp to create havoc and stampede all of the pack mules.

Joseph had calculated with great precision and pulled out at just the right moment with three companies of cavalry in pursuit. The rest of his Nez Perce warriors were waiting and hit the cavalry head on as well as on both flanks. Two companies managed to withdraw, but the third was cut off and surrounded in a lava bed, where it fought for its life until Howard and his reorganized command arrived.

The Nez Perce passed though Yellowstone National Park in late August and then turned north from Wyoming to cross Montana on their way to Canada. Howard was still in pursuit, and telegraphed orders had brought more forces into the fray: the 5th Cavalry from the Little Bighorn country and six companies of the 7th Cavalry from Fort Keogh. Under the command of Colonel Samuel D. Sturgis, the 7th Cavalry pushed up the Yellowstone River.

Wrongly informed by his scouts that there was a large cavalry force (in fact only a small detachment under Lieutenant Hugh L. Scott) on the tribe's line of advance, Joseph started a time-consuming detour before coming back to his planned line. Finally, he could avoid battle no longer, and on September 13 fought 350 of Howard's and Sturgis's cavalrymen at Canyon Creek, where the Nez Perce held the high ground. The army stormed the ridge against a hail of rifle fire and lost only three men killed while capturing 900 Indian ponies and killing 29

Nez Perces. Yet, the soldiers and their horses were more tired than the Indians and their ponies. During the night, the Nez Perce escaped once more.

The End of the Great Nez Perce March

On September 25, the Nez Perce crossed the Missouri River and brushed aside another U.S. force at Cow Island. The tribe was now close to the Canadian frontier, but was faced with one more military obstacle; a force under Colonel N. Miles. Gathered at Fort Keogh, it included six companies (some mounted) of the 6th Infantry, two companies of the 2nd Cavalry, three companies of the 7th Cavalry, two guns, and a sizeable force of white and Indian scouts.

Receiving word from Sturgis of the Nez Perces' direction of movement, Miles moved with great speed. In just 12 days, he covered 267 miles to reach the Nez Perce encampment on Eagle Creek in the Bear Paw Mountains, on September 30.

Exhausted in body and spirit, and probably believing that his people had reached Canada, Chief Joseph was caught just short of sanctuary and sensibly decided to surrender rather than fight.

His attack began at dawn. It took the Nez Perce completely by surprise, possibly because they imagined that they were already inside Canada. Even so, they responded with their usual speed and skill. The first attack was thrown back, and all manner of implements were used to fortify the camp. A siege followed, lasting for four days until Joseph finally surrendered his weary tribe, whose food was exhausted. Joseph's message ended with the emotive words "Hear me, my chiefs, my heart is sick and sad. From where the sun now stands, I will fight no more forever."

Miles arranged food and shelter for the surviving Nez Perce, 87 warriors (40 of them wounded), 184 women, and 147 children. During its three months of movement, the tribe had covered between 1,700 and 2,000 miles and was only 25 miles from the Canadian border.

Miles promised that the tribe would be sent to a reservation in Idaho, but the government decided otherwise and sent the Nez Perce to Indian Territory,

where they were decimated by disease and the climate. Miles was appalled and worked to secure the transfer of the tribe to Idaho. In 1884, the surviving members of the tribe, including Chief Joseph, were returned to Idaho.

During this period, there were also three smaller, but nonetheless troublesome, campaigns in the northwest.

The Bannock War

In 1878, the Bannock War was caused by Bannock resistance to settlement on the Camas Prairie in Idaho. The camas root, the tribe's main source of food, was being destroyed by rooting hogs which all settlers brought with them. Leaving their reservation, Chief Buffalo Horn and his Bannocks were later joined by several hundred Payute warriors. The settlers in this thinly populated area flocked to Camp Harney, the base of a small detachment of the 21st Infantry. The fort was

One of the Cheyennes' last despairing efforts to win back territory of their own ended in a deep ravine near Fort Robinson, Nebraska, where they were killed to the last man by soldiers and backwoodsmen under the command of Captain Wessells on January 9, 1879.

Frederick Remington's illustration suggests clearly the reality of the Cheyennes' last stand near Fort Robinson.

under the command of Captain George M. Downey, who lacked the strength to do anything but defend the refugees in the fort. Brigadier general Howard pushed forces into the area as quickly as possible to prevent the creation of a confederation of northwestern tribes and then took the offensive against Buffalo Horn.

The main offensive column was led by Captain Reuben F. Bernard of the 1st Cavalry. His scouts soon found the hostiles, and Buffalo Horn was killed in a skirmish at Battle Creek. As Bernard continued his march, he met a resourceful Payute girl, Sarah Winnemucca. Her father and his men were being held unwillingly in the camp, and he had a daring plan to bring them out. She infiltrated the camp dressed as a warrior and led out her father with 75 men. Their departure was soon realized, and the Bannock warriors began a pursuit. But Sarah Winnemucca rode ahead and brought back Bernard's force in time to save the Payutes. For the rest of the war Sarah Winnemucca and her sister in law, Mattie Winnemucca, served as army scouts.

Bernard now moved against the

700-strong Bannock and Payute main force, which retreated. Bernard caught the warriors and Payutes in a box canyon on June 23, 1878. He attacked in four waves, with the cavalry of the second, third, and fourth waves picking up any men wounded or dismounted in the preceding wave. Bernard's force destroyed the Indian encampment, but rather than send his men against warriors now positioned on a bluff, Bernard called off the attack. Bernard scored another success at Pilot Rock, and the hostile warriors again pulled back.

Another column was commanded by Captain Evan Miles of the 21st Infantry, leading men from that regiment together with detachments of the 1st Cavalry and 4th Artillery. As this force was about to attack a Bannock party on July 13, a party of Umatillas rode up on its flank. Miles persuaded the newly arrived Indians that he was about to be reinforced, and they agreed to await the outcome of the forthcoming battle, in which the Bannocks were driven off by Miles's two howitzers. The Umatillas then decided to fight on the army's side.

One interesting aspect of this campaign was the involvement of ships. As a party of Bannocks attempted to cross the Columbia River, three gunboats saw them. They steamed to the attack with its weapons blazing and landed a party of marines to seize the ponies and wounded abandoned by the fleeing Bannocks.

Meanwhile, additional forces had arrived to pursue the Bannocks through southern Idaho, northeast Oregon, Montana, and Wyoming. The last warriors finally drifted away to their reservations, where they were left alone. The war had cost 80 Indian lives, as well as the deaths of 31 civilians and nine soldiers.

The Sheepeater War

In 1879, several Indians in Idaho were charged (possibly wrongly) with murder. In the spring, a band of about 150 Bannocks and Shoshones, called Sheepeaters because they hunted the mountain sheep, began to raid the valleys below their mountain hideaways, burning ranches and killing Chinese miners.

With few resources available, Howard ordered just two columns into the field. One, commanded by Bernard, included 56 men of the 1st Cavalry, while the other had 48 mounted men of the 2nd Infantry, commanded by Lieutenant Henry Catley. Bernard moved hard and fast, but found nothing. Catley found action on June 29 as his column was tracking a party through a narrow defile. The column was ambushed, but Catley managed to escape during the night after abandoning his baggage.

Bernard was later reinforced by 2nd Lieutenant E.S. Farrow with a few more cavalrymen and 20 Umatilla scouts. The supplies were inadequate for the complete force, so after a fruitless search for more food, the exhausted Bernard passed command to Farrow. With 2nd Lieutenant W.C. Brown, a few cavalrymen, and the scouts, Farrow pushed the Sheepeaters so hard that in September they tired of the campaign and surrendered.

The Ute War

Also in 1879, the Ute War in northwestern Colorado stemmed from Indian resentment of the idealism and methods, both misguided and impractical, of an Indian agent, Nathan C. Meeker. Meeker had a daughter who was a teacher; he brought her to the reservation to open a Ute school. The Utes refused to send their children to the school. When Meeker issued an order that the children were to be taught, a Ute warrior knocked Meeker down.

Now fearing for the lives of everyone at the agency, Meeker secretly sent for troops. They arrived on the side of the reservation across from the agency. When the Utes confronted him with the news, Meeker told them that the soldiers were coming to uphold peace, not to punish them. The Utes clearly did not believe Meeker and left the reservation.

The 180 soldiers of Major T.T. Thornburgh's force were three companies of the 5th Cavalry and one company of the 4th Infantry. They were fortunate to have 25 wagons carrying supplies with them. On September 29, this force crossed the Milk River and, despite the warnings of a scout, pushed forward into Red Canyon because Meeker's message had been very urgent. When the column had entered the canyon, 300 to 400 Utes attacked. The advance guard and main body were nearly cut off, Thornburgh was killed, and the only chance for survival was a fast retreat to the wagon train.

At the first sound of trouble, Lieutenant J.V.S. Paddock had corralled the wagons into a defensive loop with the river at its back. He moved the horses into the center and unloaded supplies to fill the gaps between the wagons. The men from the canyon fell back into this defensive position with the Utes on their heels.

The Utes occupied higher ground outside the wagon coral and poured rifle fire down into the defenders. They set fire to the sagebrush outside the wagons, but the soldiers were able to put out the flames that reached the wagons. At dusk, the Indians charged to within 40 yards of the perimeter, but were then driven back. Four riders were sent to get help. It was not a moment too soon: the Utes now concentrated their fire on the cavalry horses and mules. Soon, more than 300 had been killed, leaving only five still alive. Most of the dead animals were used to strengthen the barricades, and as the situation became more critical, the corpses of dead soldiers were used for the same purpose.

Private Murphy covered 170 miles in 24 hours to call reinforcements, and on October 2, a relief force of one company of the 9th Cavalry, under the command of Captain Francis S. Dodge, drove through the Ute line and entered the besieged position.

Even so, the Utes were not worried and maintained their effort with a fusillade against the newcomers' horses. Soon the besieged soldiers had only seven horses left alive.

Word of the Ute rising had meanwhile reached Colonel Merritt at Fort Russell, Wyoming. He rapidly loaded 200 cavalry, 150 infantry, and some light wagons onto a train. Merritt's force disembarked at Rawlings and with the infantry located in the wagons, headed for the scene of the

action as fast as it could. The force covered a remarkable 160 miles in two days, and to the sound of the "Officers' Call" as a recognition signal, it raced through the Utes to relieve the beleaguered force by the river.

The Army now headed for the agency. On their way, they found a massacred wagon train; at the agency were the mutilated bodies of Meeker and his male assistants. The women had been carried off by the Utes, but were recovered with assistance of Chief Ouray, who had been away on a hunt as these tragic events unfolded.

The Utes were moved to a reservation in Utah. Only those who had mistreated the captured women were punished, and imprisoned at Fort Leavenworth.

War with the Navajos and Apaches in the Southwest

The third region caught up in the Indian Wars after the Civil War was the South-

The battles of the Apache Wars.

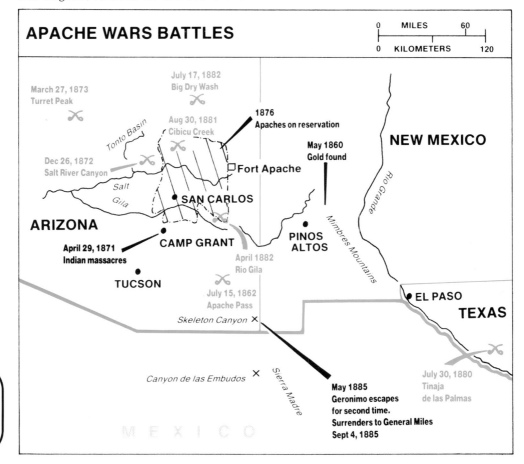

APACHE WARS BATTLES

0   MILES   60
0   KILOMETERS   120

March 27, 1873
Turret Peak

July 17, 1882
Big Dry Wash

1876
Apaches on reservation

May 1860
Gold found

NEW MEXICO

Aug 30, 1881
Cibicu Creek

Tonto Basin

Dec 26, 1872
Salt River Canyon

Salt

Gila

Fort Apache

SAN CARLOS

Rio Grande

ARIZONA

CAMP GRANT

PINOS ALTOS

Mimbres Mountains

April 29, 1871
Indian massacres

April 1882
Rio Gila

TUCSON

July 15, 1862
Apache Pass

Skeleton Canyon ✕

• EL PASO

TEXAS

Canyon de las Embudos ✕

Sierra Madre

May 1885
Geronimo escapes
for second time.
Surrenders to General Miles
Sept 4, 1885

July 30, 1880
Tinaja
de las Palmas

M E X I C O

west. The Apaches and Navajos, who ranged over Arizona and New Mexico, reacted to the intrusion of the settlers. The Apaches were the more troublesome of the two; despite their small numbers, they tied down sizeable forces for many years in an operational area that embraced not just Arizona and New Mexico, but also western Texas and the northern provinces of Mexico.

The Navajo problem was solved comparatively early. The tribe had begun to cause trouble when the first settlers arrived in 1846. In July 1863, Brigadier General James Henry Carleton, commanding the Department of New Mexico, ordered the Navajo tribe to move onto a reservation in northern Arizona and New Mexico. It was virtually inevitable that the Navajos would refuse. Carleton selected a celebrated Indian fighter, Colonel Christopher "Kit" Carson, as commander of

a force to impose the government's will on the Navajos. Carson's force contained 736 volunteer cavalry; in a clever campaign, Carson drove the Navajos back to their stronghold at Canyon de Chelly in Arizona in January, 1864. Here the cavalry laid siege to the Indians, and by the end of 1864, some 8,000 of them had surrendered for the "Long Walk" to the reservation near Fort Sumner, New Mexico. The last resistance of the tribe was broken in 1865 and 1866, and by the end of '66, the Navajos had settled on the reservation, where they remained peacefully.

The Campaign of Cochise and Mangas Coloradas

The Apaches were a much more irritating thorn in the side of settlement in the southwest, and the Apache Wars

The rugged nature of Apache country can be seen in this contemporary photograph of the entrance to Cochise's stronghold in the Dragoon Mountains.

lasted from 1861 to 1886. Until 1860, the Apaches had concentrated their efforts on the Mexicans rather than the Americans. But in 1860, gold was discovered in the Mimbres Mountains east of Pinos Altos, New Mexico, and the arrival of larger numbers of prospectors and settlers was too much for the Apaches. In 1861, two Apache leaders, Chief Cochise of the Chiricahua Apaches and his father-in-law, Chief Mangas Coloradas of the Warm Springs Apaches, started a series of raids north of the Mexican-American border. The event that sparked the first raid was an accusation of kidnapping made against Cochise in February, 1861. In reality, the Apaches were spoiling for trouble against the "invaders." Throughout 1860 and 1861, the two leaders organized a series of hit-and-run raids that resulted in many deaths and spread terror throughout Arizona and New Mexico.

On January 17, 1863, Mangas Coloradas was captured and was later murdered in prison. The loss of his father-in-law did much to persuade Cochise not to press his guerrilla raid so bitterly, but the campaign nonetheless continued intermittently through the Civil War and for five years afterward, when volunteer and regular forces lacked both the intelligence and mobility to trap this skillful warrior.

The trouble flared again in 1871 after an unprovoked attack on a village of peaceful Aravaipa Apaches outside Camp Grant. The commanding officer, Lieutenant Royal E. Whitman, had begun a promising experiment in teaching farming skills to the Apaches. While most of the fort's garrison was away on a scouting mission, a group of settlers and Papago Indians claimed that they had followed a trail from the scene of an Apache raid to the Aravaipa village, and

A bullock train of supplies on the slow move from Wilcox, Arizona, to the desperately inadequate Indian lands of the San Carlos Reservation in about 1885.

Above: Infantry and wagons cross the San Carlos River, Arizona, in about 1885.

Right: The army employed white as well as Apache scouts in the Apache wars. This 1886 photograph of Frank Bennet, a scout for the 6th Cavalry Regiment, provides a striking image of such men.

Opposite: "Micky Free," a typical scout and interpreter of the Apache wars.

on April 29, they massacred virtually the whole village. The only survivors, in fact, were a few fast runners and about 20 children who were carried off for sale in Mexico.

The Apaches immediately responded with brutal raids against ranches and small settlements, and bloody massacres of wagon trains. The army retaliated as best it could, but the problems it had faced in the 1860s were still there, now made more acute by the army's smaller numbers and the larger area covered by the Apache raiders.

General Crook Enters the Scene

In 1871, Brevet Brigadier General George Crook was appointed to head the Department of Arizona. Crook was an officer of great energy, who soon proved himself to be both an implacable opponent of the Apaches on the battlefield and their dedicated friend off the battlefield. Among Crook's other skills were organization and logical examination of any problem. As a result,

he soon created a number of highly mobile strike forces at strategic locations. Headed by officers with frontier experience and supported by trains of pack mules, these strike forces were prepared for a concerted search and destroy campaign.

The efficiency of these strike forces was greatly boosted by the enlistment of large numbers of Indian scouts, who had been authorized by a congressional act of 1866. Crook made it part of his policy to enlist some of his scouts from friendly tribes, such as the Crow and Pawnees, and others from friendly groups within the warring Apache tribes.

Crook first tried to negotiate with the Apaches, but the effort was a complete failure. One meeting was arranged with the Mojave Apaches at Camp Date Creek, but the Indians planned treachery. They reasoned that the death of the soldiers' "chief" would prevent the campaign against the Apaches, but Crook had been warned. His aide, Lieutenant William J. Ross, knocked down the barrel of the carbine that was to kill the general, and the two officers' "escort" of armed

A cavalry camp near Fort Thomas, Arizona, during 1885. Note the shelters of brushwood over the tents to provide a measure of relief from the devastating heat of the sun.

mule packers overwhelmed most of the warriors.

The Actions of Salt River Canyon and Turret Butte

War was now inevitable, and Crook began his campaign on November 15, 1872, with a sweep through the Tonto Basin. Obeying Crook's instructions to hang on to the trail of hostile parties under all circumstances, a battalion of the 5th Cavalry under Major William H. Brown finally discovered a band of Apaches in Salt River Canyon on December 26, 1872. The Apaches were holed up in a cave, and Brown led his dismounted cavalry, laden with extra ammunition and rations carried in blankets around their shoulders, in a night climb of the cliffs on the sides of the canyon. The following morning, the fighting began, and it ended only when men of Captain James Burns's column arrived. They scaled the cliffs to a point above the Apaches and then rolled boulders down onto them. The fight cost the cavalry just one man killed (a Pima scout), while the Apaches lost 74 dead and 18 prisoners.

The next operation followed an episode in which a band of Apaches attacked a group of young white men, killing all but two, who were then tied to cactus plants and shot full of arrows. Crook ordered a major effort, despite the fact that disease had crippled most of his horses and mules. Five columns were despatched, and men from Major George M. Randall's battalion of the 23rd Infantry found the Apache party on the natural fortress of Turret Butte. The Apache position appeared impregnable, but, at night and under strict orders to keep quiet, the infantry scaled the butte. At dawn on March 27, 1873, the infantrymen overran the Apaches, some of whom threw themselves to their deaths rather than face capture.

Crook maintained such pressure wherever and whenever the Apaches struck. During the spring and summer of 1874, the year in which Cochise died, there was a gradual flow of exhausted Apaches onto the reservations. Crook knew that improved living conditions would help to keep them from raiding, and he set up projects to teach them farming and shepherding. At the same time, he improved the defenses of Arizona, building roads, improving army posts, and erecting 700 miles of telegraph lines. In recognition of his work in Arizona, Crook was promoted to brigadier general (one of only five in the army of the period), but in 1875, he was posted north to the Department of the Platte, where trouble with the Sioux was brewing.

Crook's Good Work Is Undone

Crook's peace did not survive long after the departure of its author. The interests of greedy settlers came first, and several groups of incompatible Apaches were transferred in 1876 to the large but unhealthy San Carlos Reservation in the Arizona lowlands, which freed their original reservations for exploitation by newcomers.

The Campaigns of Victorio and Nana

Some of the Apache leaders refused to allow their bands to be moved. In 1877, one such man, Chief Victorio, led 100 Chiricahua and Warm Springs Apache warriors into a protracted campaign of raids. Rampaging through Arizona, New Mexico, and Texas, Victorio's band proved incredibly elusive. Pursued by veterans of the 3rd, 4th, 6th, 9th, and 10th Cavalry as well as by the Texas Rangers and groups of cowboys, Victorio's band frequently rode its horses literally to death, in a way that the cavalrymen could not, and then seized fresh mounts at the next ranch they raided. On a few occasions, he was nearly trapped, but the Apache leader seemed unworried by losses and always managed to slip away.

His favorite refuge was Mexico, where Victorio allowed the ranchers and villagers to live, on condition that they supplied him with ammunition and food as he rested. On one occasion, when

The most infamous of the Apache leaders in the Southwest was Geronimo, a legendary figure seen here, in a 1904 photograph, after he had settled down.

the Mexican authorities decided to move against him, Victorio ambushed and totally destroyed the Mexican column, and then did exactly the same to a second column.

It was inevitable that Victorio would be caught, and eventually a combined American and Mexican force tracked him into a box canyon in the Tres Castillos Mountains of northern Mexico. With everything ready for the final assault on the trapped Apaches, the Mexican commander ordered the American troops to return to the United States on the excuse that their Apache scouts might change sides. International law compelled the

Americans to comply, and the Mexicans then wiped out Victorio and all his band on October 16, 1880, in the Canyon de las Embudos.

This was not the end, for Victorio's subchief, Nana, and three other warriors were off on a small raid when Victorio met his death. Other dissident Apaches congregated around Nana, who despite his age of 70 became even more of a problem than Victorio had been. Between July 1881 and April 1882, Nana stormed 1,000 miles through the southern United States in an orgy of destruction and death. Nana's band fought eight battles with pursuing American troops and then

The Indians' struggles in the western part of the United States against the encroaching settlers were not the only battles fought to preserve traditional ways of life. There were also the quarrelsome conflicts of tribe against tribe; this illustration depicts one episode from this conflict, the assassination in 1882 of Chief Big Mouth by a rival, Chief Spotted Tail.

retired into Mexico to join forces with Geronimo.

Lesser Apache chiefs were another constant source of trouble, but in the early 1880s, the most threatening development seemed to be the emergence of a medicine man named Nock-ay-del-Klinne, who claimed that he would be able to raise the Apache dead once the settlers had been driven from the tribal lands. The arrest of the medicine man was ordered in August 1881, and Colonel E. Carr set off to implement the order with two companies of the 6th Cavalry under Captain E.C. Hentig and one company of Apache scouts under Lieutenant Thomas Cruse.

Medicine Man at Cibicu Creek

The medicine man was duly arrested on August 30 at San Carlos Reserva-tion, and the soldiers started back to the post. During a halt at Cibicu (now Cibecue) Creek, an attack was launched by the Apaches. As Cruse had suspected might happen when matters of the super-natural were involved, the army's Indian scouts mutinied and joined the attack-ing Apaches. Sergeant MacDonald had been ordered to kill the medicine man rather than let him be rescued, and just before he was himself killed, he shot the medicine man in the head. Trumpeter Ahren then put another two bullets into the medicine man's head.

Carr controlled the defense with great coolness, and the attack was driven off. But, as the dead were being buried, Ser-geant John A. Smith saw the medicine man crawling away. To avoid alerting the Apaches, Smith finally killed the medicine man with two blows of an axe. During the night, Carr moved his command toward

Fort Apache, which had been isolated by the destruction of its telegraph lines and was under Apache siege. When the siege was lifted, three of the mutinous scouts were hanged, and the others were sent to Alcatraz.

Even so, several bands of Apaches continued their raids. One band under Chief Loco was finally tracked down in April 1882 by Lieutenant Colonel G. Forsyth with four companies of the 4th Cavalry. While the main body was watering its horses from a special railroad tank car, the Indians were discovered by Lieutenant D.N. McDonald's scouting party in the Horseshoe Canyon of Stein's Peak Mountains. McDonald managed to send a messenger off before being surrounded by the Apaches, and this man killed his mount in a long gallop to find Forsyth. The colonel immediately ordered his men to McDonald's rescue, and the four companies galloped 16 miles in time to rescue McDonald without losing a horse. During the night, the Apaches escaped to Mexico, where they were intercepted. Most of their women and children were killed by the Mexican 6th Infantry Regiment in a canyon ambush.

Another outbreak of trouble in July, 1882, saw 14 companies of the 3rd and 6th Cavalry put into the field for a converging attack by three columns. One, commanded by Captain Adna R. Chaffee, caught the Apache band at Chevelon's Fork of the Little Colorado River. Another mountain climb put the soldiers in advantageous positions, and in a bitter fight the Apaches lost 16 killed and many wounded before retreating to the reservation. Chaffee's column lost two killed and seven wounded.

The Return of Crook

In 1882, the government finally decided that the main problem lay with the administration of Indian affairs and ordered the highly respected Brevet Major General Crook back to Arizona. Crook rebuilt the system of military strength and civil administration that had proved successful in the early 1870s. Pursuits of the dwindling number of hostile Apaches were pressed as vigorously as before and co-

Opposite Top: Men of the 8th Cavalry Regiment during horse training in the period between 1885 and 1900. Even with the Indian wars effectively over, the U.S. Army maintained significant forces in the west against the possibility of further uprisings.

Opposite Below: General Crook was a determined and effective foe of troublesome Indians but also a steadfast and practical friend to those whom he had pacified.

Seen in an 1890 photograph, Geronimo was really called Goyathlay. He was born in 1829 and died in 1909.

operation with the Mexicans was improved. At the same time, Crook made sure that the Indian agencies operated justly and took his life into his hands to enter the mountains and negotiate with Apache leaders.

The Campaign of Geronimo

The most important of these leaders were Geronimo, Natchez, and Chato of the Chiricahua Apaches. Geronimo had left the San Carlos Reservation in August, 1881, with 500 warriors to raid from a base in the Sierra Madre Mountains of northern Mexico. Crook got permission to cross the Mexican frontier and attacked in the late summer of 1883. After several fights, the Apaches started to surrender: the first group contained 285 warriors, while Geronimo and the others followed in September.

Infuriated by the appalling administration

Geronimo and other Apache leaders at Government Hill in San Antonio, Texas, in 1890.

General Miles and his staff on September 8, 1886.

In 1886, Geronimo was finally tracked down and pinned by a flying column of the 4th Cavalry Regiment led by Captain H.W. Lawton.

of the reservation, Geronimo escaped once more in May, 1885. Crook arranged a parley in March, 1886, and finally persuaded Geronimo to surrender on the agreement that the Apache warriors and their families should not be separated, and that if they were sent east it should be for a period no longer than two years. During the night, a bootlegger named Tribollet plied the Apache camp with mescal. After indulging in this strong liquor, Geronimo and some of his closest supporters fled the camp. Crook reported the matter to Lieutenant General Sheridan, commanding general of the army, and Sheridan demanded that the surrender terms be renegotiated since Geronimo had disappeared. Crook asked to be relieved, and on April 2, he was succeeded by Brigadier General Miles. Miles was a supporter of Crook's methods and sent Lieutenant

Geronimo and other Apaches await movement into captivity after their final surrender in 1886.

Charles B. Gatewood into the mountains to confer with Geronimo, who finally surrendered at Skeleton Canyon on September 4, 1886. The Indian Wars of the southwest were finally over.

The Ghost Dance War

The last act of the Indian Wars was played out in the north, where Chief Sitting Bull had never been content with the peace imposed on the Sioux and their allied tribes. After the 1876 campaign and the Battle of the Little Bighorn, they had lost the Black Hills region, and the treaty that ended the Sioux War in 1877 had reduced their remaining lands by half and driven a wedge of homesteaded land into them.

In 1889, eight years after the last northern bands had been confined to their reservations, a Payute shaman named Wovoda emerged in Nevada. Wovoda was the creator of a mystical religious movement known as the Ghost Dance cult. It promised a new world, in which the Indians would be reunited with their dead and the lost buffalo herds in a place free of pain, hunger, and, most important of all, the white man. The beliefs and rituals of the cult centered on the Ghost Dance, in which the Ghost Shirt was worn, and emphasized peace. Soon, the more martial of the Sioux tribes, and in particular the Tetons, adapted the cult to a military purpose and claimed that the Ghost Shirt was bulletproof. Depressed Indians of many reservations throughout Montana, Wyoming, Nebraska, the Dakotas, Texas, and Oklahoma adopted the cult rapidly and fervently.

Despite their hunger, the Sioux began selling their ration cattle to buy rifles and ammunition. In these circumstances, the authorities soon felt that the Pine Ridge and Rosebud reservations were on the verge of rebellion.

The catalyst for the trouble was Sitting Bull, who was located at the Standing Rock Agency. He broke his peace pipe and, in the presence of Ghost Dancers, declared his willingness to fight for the new religion that promised the deaths of all whites. General Miles sent ''Buffalo Bill'' Cody to arrest Sitting Bull, but the agent realized that this move would inevitably spark trouble. On December 14, 1890, he entrusted the task to 40 Indian police under Lieutenant Bull Head.

When Sitting Bull was arrested, he called out for rescue, and one of his followers shot Bull Head. Two of the policemen then shot and killed Sitting Bull, and a fierce fight broke out between the police and 160 Ghost Dancers. Only after the arrival of Captain E.G. Fetchet and two troops of the 8th Cavalry did the Ghost Dancers flee.

Brigadier General J. R. Rooke, com-

manding the department, decided to concentrate his strength at the Pine Ridge Agency, Nebraska, and despatched a column of cavalry under Colonel E.V. Sumner to catch some of Sitting Bull's followers, a party led by Big Foot of the Mineconjou Sioux. Sumner soon intercepted Big Foot and received the Indian chief's surrender. Knowing the delicacy of the situation, Sumner did not disarm and surround the Indian party, but instead allowed it to camp overnight before returning to the reservation the following day.

Sumner was too trustful; during the night, Big Foot's party slipped away and headed for the Badlands. Sumner pursued them, and other army forces were also on the hunt. The 9th Cavalry and a platoon from Light Battery E of the 1st Artillery blocked one of the Indian party's possible lines of movement, while four troops of the 7th Cavalry, another platoon of the 1st Artillery's Light Battery E, and Troop A of the Indian Scouts covered another avenue.

The death of Sitting Bull on December 14, 1890.

The man who shot
Sitting Bull was Red
Tomahawk, an Indian
policeman of the
Standing Rock
Reservation.

An Indian scout attached to Major S.M. Whitside's detachment of the 7th Cavalry located Big Foot's party on December 28. Soon Whitside's force had closed up on the Indians. The Indian party included women and children, but the men were stripped to breechclouts and leggings, covered with war paint, and well equipped with Winchester repeating rifles. The Indians formed line and advanced against the cavalry, but Whitside rode to meet them and asked them to surrender. Big Foot, who was ill with pneumonia and traveling in a wagon, arrived and again surrendered as his party was outnumbered, cold, and without food.

The Battle of Wounded Knee Creek

Whitside's detachment escorted the Indian party back to his camp at Wounded Knee Creek, about 14 miles northeast of Pine Ridge Agency. The soldiers provided

Big Foot's band just before a grass dance near the Cheyenne River on August 9, 1890. Nearly all these men were killed in the Battle of Wounded Knee.

food for the Sioux, who numbered 120 men and 230 women and children. Whitside had earlier sent a report of Big Foot's surrender to the Agency, and Colonel James W. Forsyth with four more troops of the 7th Cavalry and three more 1.65-inch Hotchkiss guns of Light Battery E of the 1st Artillery under the command of Captain Allyn Capron arrived at the creek.

They spent the night quietly and the Sioux were apparently in good spirits. At dawn, the Indians prepared to move. Forsyth arranged some of his men in a ring around the Indians to discourage any attempt at flight. Forsyth had been ordered to disarm the Indians; after he issued his orders, the Indians surrendered a few old and broken weapons, claiming that they were the only ones they had.

Forsyth ordered a search. Soon, the soldiers found weapons hidden by the Sioux women, who had been moved away from the men for safety in case there was trouble.

Exactly what happened next remains uncertain. Accounts vary, but the most likely event is that a medicine man reminded the warriors that their Ghost Shirts were bullet proof, and that this persuaded 120 warriors to chance themselves against 470 encircling soldiers. The spark was a single shot fired by a warrior; the result was the Battle of Wounded Knee, a bloody stand-up in which the soldiers tried to close in on the Indians. The two troops who had been supervising the warriors were armed with single-shot Springfields and could not check a break for open ground by the Sioux with their repeating rifles. The two troops lost nine men killed and 11 wounded as the Indians broke out of the encircling fire that had spread to the Indian camp.

The fleeing Sioux were fired on by the Hotchkiss guns, which took a terrible toll of human and horse flesh, and Forsyth then directed the army's effort against the sole surviving party, who were making a

Above: The Sioux included a large number of tribes, including the Assinniboines, seen here in a group at the time of the end of the Sioux wars.

Right: A mule-borne litter carries a casualty from the Battle of Wounded Knee.

Above: Collecting the dead after the Battle of Wounded Knee.

Left: The frozen body of Chief Big Foot at the site of the Battle of Wounded Knee.

stand at the head of a gully about half a mile down the ravine of Wounded Knee Creek.

Six hours after the start of the fighting, it was all over. The Sioux lost 145 men, women, and children killed, as well as another 33 wounded. The army losses were 25 killed and 37 wounded.

The 7th Cavalry returned swiftly to the Pine Ridge Agency with its prisoners, as well as with all the wounded. One more Sioux band was still on the run, however, and six troops were detached to hunt it down. They completed their task with minimal bloodshed the following day at White Clay Creek.

There were still several thousand Sioux on the loose, and Miles flooded the area with men of the 6th, 7th, 8th, and 9th Cavalry as well as the 2nd and 21st Infantry, during the winter of 1890-91. Harried and manifestly not receiving the supernatural aid they had been promised, the Sioux were steadily herded back to their reservations. The last Sioux surrendered on January 15, 1891. The Sioux wars were over.

Above: The return of Major James S. Cassey's detachment from the Battle of Wounded Knee where the detachment cleared the key bluff on the army's left after making a difficult ascent in their buffalo overcoats in the face of plunging fire from the Sioux on the summit and killed Chief Big Crow, the Indians broke and left this commanding site to the Americans.

There were still a few small episodes to follow, but they fell into the category of civil disturbance rather than war. The last two incidents occurred between October 4 and 7, 1897, when a detachment of the 3rd Infantry suppressed a troublesome group of disaffected Chippewas at Leech Lake, Minnesota, and in 1906, when 400 Utes left their reservation and terrorized an area of Wyoming.

The Indian Wars had turned the U.S. Army into a superb fighting force, man for man equal to, indeed superior to, any army in the world in the skills of irregular warfare. The morality of the seizure of Indian lands will continue to be debated, but it is worth noting that, in 1924, American citizenship was at last granted to all native-born Indians in the United States.

Above: The most abiding popular image of the Indian wars is an attack on a wagon train by Indian tribesmen of the Great Plains.

Left: This camp near the Pine Ridge Reservation, South Dakota, held the largest concentration of native Americans in the United States when it was photographed on January 16, 1891.

Glossary

Battalion Basic organizational and tactical subdivision of a regiment in the period before the Civil War. Generally not used in the Civil War, except in federal heavy artillery regiments retrained as infantry, which were made up of three four-company battalions, each commanded by a major.

Battery Basic organizational and tactical subdivision of an artillery regiment, corresponding to the company in an infantry regiment.

Blockade Naval operation designed to deny the enemy the use of his ports. Regular patrols try to intercept warships or merchant shipping attempting to enter or leave anywhere along the blockaded coast.

Boom Barrier across a waterway to prevent enemy movements.

Brigade Tactical grouping of two or more regiments. In the Civil War, an average brigade was made up of about five regiments. At the Battle of Chancellorsville, the Federal brigades averaged 4.7 regiments with about 2,000 men, while the Confederate brigades averaged 4.5 regiments with about 1,840 men.

Cartridge Complete round of ammunition, with the powder and projectile in a container to simplify carrying and loading.

Collier Ship designed to carry coal.

Column Body of troops with the units arranged one behind the other.

Cordon defense Area defense provided by bodies of troops strung out along the "frontier" of a region to detect and attack any enemy force seeking to break into the defended region.

Corps Operational grouping of two or more divisions. In the Civil War, a corps averaged about three divisions. The standard organization of the Federal corps was 45 infantry regiments and nine batteries of light artillery.

Division Operational grouping of two or more brigades. In the Civil War, a division averaged three brigades. At the Battle of Chancellorsville, the Federal divisions averaged 6,200 officers and men, while Confederate divisions averaged 8,700 officers and men.

Entrenchment Improvised defensive positions made by digging a hole or trench and mounding the excavated earth in front of the hole to provide above-ground protection.

Frigate Basic warship of the Federal navy, designed to fight other warships, but also to undertake commerce-raiding operations.

Intelligence Organization of information about the enemy's plans, movements, strengths, and dispositions.

Invest Take under siege.

Bibliography

Ambrose, Stephen E. *Crazy Horse and Custer: The Parallel Lives of Two American Warriors.* (Doubleday & Co., Garden City, NY, 1975).

Andris, Ralph K, *The Long Death: The Last Days of the Plains Indian.* (Macmillan, New York, 1964).

Athearn, Robert. *William Tecumseh Sherman and the Settlement of the West.* (University of Oklahoma Press, Norman, OK, 1956).

Beal, Merrill D. *I Will Fight No More Forever: Chief Joseph and the Nez Perce War.* (Ballantine Books, New York, 1975).

Bourke, Cyrus Townsend. *Indian Fights and Fighters.* (University of Nebraska, Lincoln, NE, 1971). Colorful popular history.

Brown, Dee Alexander. *Bury My Heart At Wounded Knee: An Indian History of the American West.* (Holt, Rinehart & Winston, New York, 1971).

Chalfant, William Y. *Cheyennes and Horse Soldiers.* (University of Oklahoma, Norman, OK, 1989).

Connnell, Evan S. *Son of the Morning Star.* (North Point Press, San Francisco, CA, 1984). The best biography of Custer.

Debo, Angie. *Geronimo: The Man, His Time, His Place.* (University of Oklahoma Press, Norman, OK, 1977).

Dunlay, Thomas W. *Wolves for the Blue Soldiers.* (University of Nebraska, Lincoln, NE, 1982). The role of the Indian scouts who guided the national army against their people.

Hutton, Paul Andrew. *Phil Sheridan and His Army.* (University of Nebraska Press, Lincoln, NE, 1973). Covers Indian wars on the Great Plains involving Sheridan's Army.

McNitt, Frank. *Navajo Wars.* (University of New Mexico, 1972).

Marrin, Albert. *War Clouds in the West.* (Atheneum, New York, 1984). For younger readers.

Trafzer, Clifford E. *The Kit Carson Campaign: The Last Great Navajo War.* (University of Oklahoma, Norman, OK, 1982).

Utley, Robert M. and Wilcomb E. Washburn. *The American Heritage History of the Indian Wars.* (American Heritage Publishing Co., New York, 1977).

Utley, Robert M. *Frontier Regulars: The United States Army and the Indian 1866-1891.* (Macmillan, New York, 1973).

Utley, Robert M. (ed.). *Life in Custer's Cavalry.* (Yale University Press, New Haven, CT, 1977). Eyewitness accounts.

Index

Page numbers in *Italics* refer
to illustration